T0057320

Some Assembly Required

The Not-So-Secret Life
of a Transgender Teen

ARIN ANDREWS

with JOSHUA LYON

SIMON & SCHUSTER BFYR

NEW YORK   LONDON   TORONTO   SYDNEY   NEW DELHI

SIMON & SCHUSTER BFYR

An imprint of Simon & Schuster Children's Publishing Division

1230 Avenue of the Americas, New York, New York 10020

SIMON & SCHUSTER BFYR is a trademark of Simon & Schuster, Inc.

For information about special discounts for bulk purchases, please contact Simon & Schuster Special
Sales at 1-866-506-1949 or business@simonandschuster.com.

The Simon & Schuster Speakers Bureau can bring authors to your live event. For more information
or to book an event, contact the Simon & Schuster Speakers Bureau at 1-866-248-3049 or visit our
website at www.simonspeakers.com.

Book design by Laurent Linn

The text for this book is set in Aldine 401.

Manufactured in the United States of America

2 4 6 8 10 9 7 5 3 1

Library of Congress Cataloging-in-Publication Data

Andrews, Arin.

Some assembly required : the not-so-secret life of a transgender teen / Arin Andrews.

pages cm

Summary: "Seventeen-year-old Arin Andrews shares all the hilarious, painful, and poignant details of
undergoing gender reassignment as a high school student in this winning teen memoir"— Provided by
publisher.

ISBN 978-1-4814-1675-7 (hardback) — ISBN 978-1-4814-1677-1 (e-book) 1. Andrews, Arin—Juvenile
literature. 2. Transsexual youth—United States—Biography—Juvenile literature. 3. Transgender youth—
United States—Biography—Juvenile literature. 4. Transgenderism—United States—Juvenile literature.
I. Title.

HQ77.8.A53A3 2014   306.76'80835—dc23   2014010948

FIRST
EDITION

For my mom:

Thank you for loving me endlessly and giving me life,

not once but twice.

I love you.

1

Getting dumped at prom sucks.

I mean, getting dumped *period* sucks, obviously. But to have it happen in formal wear in front of hundreds of people adds a humiliating slap across the face that an I-just-want-to-be-friends text can't compete with.

It's basically the exact opposite of being voted prom king. In fact, it feels like the prom king decided to have you executed.

It's not like there weren't warning signs that the night was going to be a disaster. I'd met my date, Jessica, during the second semester of my sophomore year of high school, when I was still going by my female birth name, Emerald. She was bi, and I was out as gay at the time. I never referred to myself as a lesbian, just gay. "Lesbian" would have implied that I was a girl who liked girls.

I knew that I was a boy who liked girls.

My friend Alyssa introduced me to Jessica—we were all

in the same psychology class. Alyssa is the type of girl who likes to touch. She was always hugging me and holding on for just a little too long, but not in a flirty way. She's just physically affectionate. Jessica was a little more removed. She had this aloof, ice princess quality that I'd always thought was kind of sexy. Leading up to the prom, we'd never dated or anything, though; I was always too shy to ask her out. So when prom came around and her friends were all taking it way too seriously for Jessica's taste, with limo rentals and elaborate invitations written in soap on a prospective date's car, I was beyond psyched when she asked me to take her.

"We'll make it a good time," she promised me.

Oh, yes we will, I thought, imagining us slow dancing under swirling lights.

I had started the very first steps of transitioning from female to male shortly after meeting Jessica. According to the standards of care within the medical community, I needed to live in public as a male for one year before I would be allowed to have any kind of gender reassignment surgery, like having my breasts removed. I began to ask people to call me Arin instead of Emerald, and to refer to me as "he" instead of "she." For the most part Jessica was cool about it, but every now and then she'd start whining: "Why can't you just be gay? Why do you have to mess with this whole transgender thing? Why can't you be normal?"

She considered herself something of a rebel, but I think my coming out as trans was one step too far over the line for her. Bisexual was edgy, gay was even cooler, but being transgender was a new one for most of the people in our school. But that was okay with me at first—I understood that a lot of people were going to have a hard time getting used to the change, and I naively didn't let her complaints upset me. I thought I could educate her.

Also, to be perfectly honest, she was two years older, and it was kind of a big deal for a sophomore like me to get to attend prom.

I spent hours getting ready the night of the dance. When I had been Emerald, if I'd needed to dress for a formal event, I'd throw on whatever hideous dress my mom had picked out for the occasion, and I'd invariably end up letting her brush my hair since I couldn't be bothered myself. She loved to do it, though. She took any and every opportunity I gave her to try to make me look pretty. Mom named me after the Emerald Pool at Trafalgar Falls in Dominica—she had visited there while pregnant with me and thought it was the most beautiful place she'd ever seen. It was a lot to try to live up to back then.

But for my first prom as Arin, I went all out. I discovered the color of Jessica's dress and bought a blue shirt to wear with my suit so we'd match. I ironed all my clothes until the creases were razor sharp, and I polished my black dress shoes until I could see my reflection in them. I spent forever in the shower, scrubbing myself clean. After I toweled off and put on my binder—a tight piece of elastic that squashes your boobs to give the appearance of a flat chest—I messed with my hair for at least twenty minutes until I got it just right.

It hadn't even occurred to me to buy a corsage, until my

mom told me she'd be pissed if her prom date showed up without one, so we stopped at a florist shop on our way to Jessica's house. I chose a white rose on a wristband for her, and a matching boutonnière for me.

"Promise me you won't drink," Mom lectured.

"I won't," I said.

"And don't get into a car if anyone else has been drinking."

"I *won't*," I said. I wished she'd just trust me. I had no interest in partying. All I wanted was to be out in the world as a boy with a beautiful girl on my arm. I wasn't about to ruin that feeling with booze.

She dropped me off in front of Jessica's and leaned over to kiss my cheek.

"You look very handsome," she said, and reached out to ruffle my hair. I ducked her hand.

"Don't touch it," I said. "This took forever!"

We locked eyes for a moment. The past few years had been the worst of our lives. I'd come back from wanting to die. Initially she had vehemently resisted my need to transition, and if you'd told me even four months prior that we'd be experiencing this moment together—me with short hair, dressed in a suit, taking a girl to prom—well, I would have called you crazy.

"Love you," I said, getting out of the car and slamming the door shut behind me.

I knocked on Jessica's door, and her dad answered. I had no idea if he knew I was transgender, and I think he sensed I was nervous.

"Hello, Arin," he said, giving me a firm handshake. "Come on in. Jessica's told me all about you."

Everything? I wondered.

Jessica appeared from the hallway, fastening an earring into place.

"Hey," she said, sounding bored.

Her hair was pulled up into a pouf on top of her head, held in place with a thin circular braid. The rest curled and tumbled down past her shoulders. It was sort of a fifties retro thing, like that singer from the B-52s. Her strapless teal dress was covered in rhinestones around her breasts, and more shiny rocks marched in vertical lines toward her waist, where the cloth dissolved into layers of tulle. Her legs were bare, and ended in open-toed black heels. I thought she looked beautiful, and told her so.

"Thanks," she said, and I felt a twinge of disappointment when she didn't comment on my suit.

I slipped her corsage onto her wrist but fumbled when I tried to pin my boutonnière. Her dad saw me struggling and stepped up to help me get it on straight while Jessica watched, a slight smirk on her face. That should have been warning number one—wasn't she the one who should have been playing this part in the ritual?

But the thought disappeared when her dad finished and gave me a little pat on the shoulder. All he had to do was refer to me as "son," and it would have been a moment right out of some cheesy prom episode of a sitcom. I was going through the same motions that generations of American boys had gone through before me, and it felt unreal and incredible at the same time.

We took a few photos outside, and then piled into her dad's car to take our official prom pictures at the town gazebo. It's a Catoosa, Oklahoma, tradition, and there were at least ten other couples there jostling for a place on the steps.

As gazebos go, it's not much to look at. Plus, there are only so many angles to shoot from where you don't get a view of a gas station or the shuttered Lil' Abner's Dairyette in the background.

Afterward, we drove back to Jessica's house. Alyssa and her date, a guy named Eric whom Alyssa had been dating on and off for about a year, were pulling into the driveway in a beat-up red car—our ride for the night. Alyssa looked stunning in a really simple strapless, eggplant-colored gown. Eric, on the other hand, was in jeans and sneakers and was still buttoning up a short-sleeved plaid shirt over a long-sleeved white thermal top. His hair was a disheveled mess. I didn't know him all that well, and his appearance seemed pretty disrespectful. I shot Alyssa a questioning look, and she just rolled her eyes. *Don't ask.*

After a few more photos it was time to go. I was sort of surprised when Jessica jumped into the front seat next to Eric instead of sitting in the back with me, so Alyssa and I climbed into the cramped backseat. It still didn't occur to me that anything was wrong, though. I was just too excited. I snapped clueless selfies and posted them to Facebook, making sure that my boutonnière showed up in the shots.

Look at me, on the way to the prom! My date's in the front.

We were headed to Catoosa's fanciest restaurant—a popular Italian place—when things really started to dissolve.

"There's a party at Ryan's house after prom. We should go," Eric said. "He'll have beer."

Jessica got super-excited. "Oh, totally," she said, and turned around to face me for the first time. "Arin, you in?"

I felt my heart sink as I remembered the conversation I'd had with my mom earlier. I'd given her my word, and that meant something to me. Plus, being around a bunch of drunk teenagers isn't exactly my idea of a good time. They tend to get a little too probing with their questions about my being transgender. I enjoy talking to people about trans issues, but when alcohol gets involved, the queries inevitably end up being mostly about my genitals, and I didn't want anything to ruin this night.

"Yeah, no, I don't think that's a good idea," I said.

The mood in the car shifted almost immediately. Everyone got real quiet, until Alyssa said, "Come on. I bet it'll be fun!"

"I can't," I said. I saw everyone exchange glances with one another. I hoped that maybe they'd change their minds, but I still discreetly texted Mom that I might need a ride home after the dance. Even if they went without me afterward, I was still determined to have a good time at the prom itself.

When we got to the restaurant, I beamed when the hostess called me "sir." It was *working*. All that was missing was a hot date on my arm. I looked around for Jessica, but she was standing a few feet behind me, looking bored and unhappy.

She cheered up when we sat down and the waiter, a college-age guy with brown spiky hair, came over to our table and promptly settled his gaze on Jessica's chest.

"You guys look pretty sober for prom night," he drawled, his eyes still glued to her. "Can I interest you in some wine?"

Eric and Jessica got really excited. But just like at the gazebo earlier, half the town—including a few of our teachers—was at the restaurant.

"We'd better not," Jessica whispered to the waiter, batting her eyelashes at him. "But *thank you*."

"Suit yourself," he said, shrugging. He continued to leer at Jessica's cleavage while he took our order, and she fussed with her hair, loving the attention.

Oh well, I thought. At least my date is so hot that all the guys want her.

After dinner we headed over to the dance. Prom wasn't being held at our school. I guess the idea of having it off-site was supposed to make the night feel special, but the venue the prom committee had chosen, the Home Builders Association of Greater Tulsa, was about as glamorous as if they'd hosted the prom in a hospital cafeteria. From the outside the building looks like any other industrial office complex, and despite some silver streamers hanging from the ceiling and bunches of pink, yellow, and blue balloons taped to the walls, the banquet hall couldn't have been more bland.

At least the theme, "A Night to Remember," was appropriate.

When we walked through the front doors, all of the chaperones made a big fuss over us. They told me how handsome I looked, how beautiful Jessica was. Our high school administration had actually been really supportive of my transition—the teachers all called me Arin. I still had to use the bathroom in the nurse's office because I wasn't allowed to use the guys' room, but they at least understood that the one for girls wasn't an option for me. Everyone's enthusiasm at seeing us together made my heart swell, and for one last moment I believed that the night might be okay, that this could be the storybook prom everyone is supposed to get if they want it. I turned to Jessica to ask her if she wanted to dance, but she was saying something to Eric.

"Will you hold this for a minute?" she asked, handing him the corsage I'd bought her.

"Sure," he said, and she turned around and walked off into the crowd.

Confused, I scanned the dancing hordes and saw her standing on tiptoe, whispering something to a guy I recognized as Ryan, the one hosting the after-party. The music morphed into a new song, and they started dancing together.

I stood there staring at them, still not quite understanding what was going on.

"Come on," Alyssa said, grabbing my hand. "Let's dance. I don't know why she's being so weird."

Alyssa and I danced for a few songs. I tried to keep my eyes on Jessica, but she kept disappearing. And whenever I did see her, she was dancing with either Ryan or some other tall guy in a tux whom I didn't recognize.

I felt my phone buzz in my pocket. It was a text from a strange number.

What do you have in your pants?

I hit delete.

"Who was it?" Alyssa yelled over the music.

"Nobody," I said. I'd gotten messages like that before, and refused to engage.

A slow country love song started to play. Alyssa and Eric coupled off, and in a burst of bravado I shoved my way through the crowd, looking for Jessica. I finally saw her standing near a table stocked with gallon jugs of sweet tea and store-bought snack platters stacked high with sweaty cubes of pale pink meat and rubbery cheese. A look of panic crossed her face as I approached.

"Will you dance with me?" I asked.

"Oh, o-okay," she stammered, looking around her, as if hoping someone would come and rescue her.

We walked out into the middle of the dance floor, and I went to put my arm around her waist, but she moved back a step and reached her arms out. She put her hands on my shoulders, with about two feet of space between us, and I realized that this was going to happen junior-high style.

She refused to make eye contact with me the entire time, and the song seemed to last forever. I felt like an idiot, and was convinced that everyone in the room knew this was a pity dance on her part.

The moment the song was over, she dropped her arms, turned around, and walked away without a word.

I headed to the snack table and poured some sweet tea, utterly depressed. When I turned back to face the crowd, I saw her dancing with the tall guy in the tux. He was wearing the corsage I'd given her. She must have gotten it back from Eric.

When the lights finally came on, she made her way over to me.

"So, I'm going to catch another ride to that party," she said. The tall tux guy was standing off to one side, holding her coat.

"Great," I said, totally deadpan.

"Okay, well, bye." She suddenly tried to give me a hug.

"No, forget it," I said, taking a step back.

"Whatever," she said, rolling her eyes. She spun on her heel and took off.

Alyssa had watched the whole exchange and now rushed over.

"Oh my God, I'm so sorry. I don't know what's gotten into her," she said, hugging me.

"It's fine," I mumbled into her shoulder.

"Look, I think we're going to go to that party too," she said sheepishly. "Please come with us."

I shook my head and pulled out my phone to text Mom to come get me.

I told her what happened as soon as I got into the car.

"You're going to find someone," she promised as I sat there in the passenger seat, staring at my lap. "This was just one date, one of many you're going to go on. Some work out and some don't, but I know that there is someone out there who is perfect for you. It takes time."

Rationally I knew all of this was true. But emotionally nothing she said resonated. I woke up the next morning still angry and depressed, but a full night of sleep and a chance to really reflect on Mom's "buck up" speech seemed to be help-ing. I decided to not let what had happened at prom get to me. My attitude was basically, *Screw it. I don't care. She wasn't even that pretty.*

I scarfed down some toast and took my coffee out onto the back deck. Our house sits on the top of a steep incline that leads down into a wooded ravine. Spring was in full force, and I could hear the stream at the bottom of the hill roaring with fresh rainwater. Technically we live in Broken Arrow, a suburb of Tulsa, but our place is located about fifteen minutes from the heart of town, in the middle of the countryside.

Two of our three dogs followed me down the steps and into the woods, down a trail to my favorite pile of moss-covered boulders. The stones are ancient, and are so haphazardly placed that they look like a giant hurled them toward our house from miles away.

I scrambled up on top of them, sat down, and chucked a few pebbles off into the forest, trying to think of ways to distract myself from the previous night.

I decided to go to the weekly Saturday night dance party at the Openarms Youth Project center. OYP is basically a safe place for underage gay and trans kids to hang out, and I needed to be around people like me. OYP serves snacks and sodas, and there's a little lounge area with couches near the dance floor. There are drag shows once a month, and the center hosts their own prom every year. A staff of volunteers runs OYP, and no one older than twenty-one is allowed in. It's a great resource for the youth community, but from the outside it looks like a seedy bar, a windowless concrete structure at the end of an industrial stretch of warehouses sandwiched between a strip mall and a Baptist church. There's a small wooden porch that looks like it's just propped up against the front door as an afterthought, and a fenced-in concrete back-yard.

I was going through a preppy phase, so that night I slipped on a pair of white cargo shorts, a white button-down shirt, and some Sperrys. Mom dropped me off, and when I walked inside, I immediately spotted my friend Dale, another trans guy, sitting across the room.

"Hey! How was your prom?" he asked. "Get lucky?"

"Hardly," I said, and flopped down onto the couch beside him.

I was in the middle of filling him in on my awful night when I noticed the front door open. I glanced over and saw a girl walk in. I caught only a quick glimpse of her profile before she turned away from me. But I could tell that she was stunning. Tall, with long dark hair, and wearing a black shirt with a few sequins that caught the light, making her sparkle. She was wearing skinny jeans that hugged her butt perfectly.

I nudged Dale. "What's a gorgeous girl like that doing in a dive like this?" I joked.

At that moment she turned in my direction, and I got a look at her face. My mouth dropped open.

"Oh my God, that's Katie Hill."

Déjà vu washed over me, and I started to sweat a little.

I felt like I was hurtling back in time, to the day when I'd first read her name in the paper and learned that she was transgender, like me. Memories of when suicide had felt like my only option came creeping back in, reminding me of just how far I'd come since I'd been a little kid trying to pee standing up behind my grandparents' barn.

I had to talk to her. It felt like I'd been waiting my whole life to.

The handful of skyscrapers that make up Tulsa, Oklahoma, jut up erratically against a horizon that stretches out, smooth and wide, on both sides. It looks like someone's final heartbeat on a hospital monitor, a last-gasp attempt at life after having flatlined. The city's streets and sidewalks are often eerily quiet and empty.

But just twenty minutes away is the countryside. That's where real life begins in Oklahoma.

One of my earliest memories is of staring up into the enormous brown eyes of a cow while my arm disappeared farther and farther into her mouth. I'd been given a green protein pellet to feed her and had put it in the palm of my purple-gloved hand, instead of holding it out with my fingers like I'd been taught.

The cow's mouth had closed around my wrist, and I'd been sucked forward and up onto my toes. I was half-aware of Papa, my grandfather, yelling and running toward me, but I wasn't scared. I felt warm. Streams of clear snot ran down the cow's nose and onto my shoulder, but I wasn't grossed out. We held eye contact, and I dimly started to wonder if she was going to swallow me whole, when I suddenly felt my whole body jerk backward. As if in slow motion, I watched my arm glide out of the animal's mouth.

My hand was bare. The cow had swallowed my girly purple glove. I think on some primal level the cow and I had both known that it didn't belong there to begin with.

The farm belongs to Papa and my grandmother Gigi. It's about half an hour away from our home in Broken Arrow and sits on approximately eighty acres, with two ponds, a creek, pastures full of hay bales for jumping on, and trees that beg to be climbed. It's where Mom and her sister, my aunt Susan, grew up. Susan has six adopted children, and three of them—Dewayne, Cheyenne, and Amanda—are roughly the same age as me. We were raised like siblings, so I always had other kids to play with when I was over there. Mom was adopted as well, and I grew up implicitly understanding my grandparents' mantra: *Blood doesn't make you kin.* It's the value of the relationship that determines family.

My biological dad, a marine, took off when he found out my mom was pregnant. I've never met him, and even though we share DNA, he is in no way my father. If you have someone else who raises you and treats you as their own, like I do with my stepfather, there's no reason to think he's not your father. I don't even consider him a stepfather—he *is* my dad. The same goes with my half brother, Wesley, who's four years younger than me. I forged childhood bonds with him and my adopted cousins that make them all my full brothers and sisters.

On the farm we'd play haystack tag, where each mound represented either a hiding spot or home base. Sometimes Papa would tie a flat piece of sheet metal to the back of his pickup truck and drive us through the pastures, whipping us around as if we were in an inner tube on a lake. We'd cling on for as long as possible, until we got thrown off, tangled in one another's limbs. A yellow-brick salt lick for the cows sat in a tire in the middle of one of the fields. We'd take turns lapping at the smooth craters made by the animals' enormous, catlike tongues, and get a jolt from the delicious, sharp tang. The farm was an entire world unto itself, and it was all ours.

Sometimes there'd be a sudden shift in the wind, and the cows would take off for the cover of the trees; we'd look up and see clouds swirling and turning green. We'd run for the tornado bunker, a hunk of concrete with a hatch door rising from the ground next to the house. But even though we live smack in the heart of tornado alley, Papa and Gigi's property and the surrounding town has never been hit. Legend has it that the Cherokee blessed the land to protect it from twisters, and so far it has worked.

The only thing that ever got in the way of my outdoor life was asthma. When I have an attack, my throat rattles and makes choking sounds. I had to teach myself early on not to panic, and I carry an inhaler with me everywhere. I have bad allergies, too, which sucks for someone who loves being outside as much as I do. But a runny nose is a small price to pay for an open sky.

Though I much preferred playing outside with my cousins, my mom insisted on enrolling me at age three in dance classes at a place called Moore's Dance Studio. My first performance at a recital was a tap routine to a song called "A Baby Duck." Imagine fourteen preschoolers in canary-yellow leotards, with feathers sticking out of their hair and shoulders, all attempting a coordinated kick routine but failing miserably. We looked like tiny drunken Vegas showgirls, stumbling all over the stage. My tap movements were more like stomps, and I'd halt every few seconds to search for Mom in the audience and wave.

Dance became a huge part of my life. I took jazz, ballet, Irish step, hip-hop, and tap. But my favorite was clogging—we wore tap shoes with double clickers on the heels and toes, so the sound was extra loud. I loved learning the controlled movements, teaching my body to behave exactly the way I commanded it to.

The costumes were an entirely different story. There were white tutus with pink bunny ears, teal kimonos with silver sequined trim on the arms and layers of flouncy cotton erupting from beneath the shortened hemlines, pink-and-black-striped leotards with fishnet stockings, candy-cane-colored pants that flared at the heel.

I loathed them all.

The second we'd get home from a recital, I'd rip off the costume and slap on a pair of camo shorts and a T-shirt. I'd wrestle anyone, and none of my cousins were scared of hurting me, because they knew I could kick their butt. We'd play army, and I was always the commander, bossing everyone around and barking orders, mapping out the plans of attack against our unseen enemy.

Papa and Gigi built a big shed in their side yard for us

to play in, and hung a red sign above the front door: BUNK-HOUSE. In smaller letters under that it read NO SPITTIN' NO CUSSIN' NO FIGHTIN'. We didn't cuss, but there was plenty of the other two going on, especially when my cousins wanted to play house and I insisted on being the father. I had three names for myself that I'd rotate out each time we played—Hunter, Gunner, and Jake.

Mom wasn't really fazed by any of this. Since I was going to dance class regularly too, she considered me "well rounded." Everyone else just called me a tomboy, which I loved, because it had the word "boy" in it.

One day when I was in third grade, Papa took me out to lunch. I looked him square in the eye and announced that even though I had a father, I was old enough to be the real man of the house, and that I needed a gun to protect my family. I had no interest in hunting with one, though, because I love animals too much. Mom was always adopting stray dogs, and the woods behind our house were filled with kittens that would play among the trees. A baby skunk that had gotten lost in an ice storm lived in our kitchen for a while, and once, Mom even rescued a fawn that our neighbors' dog had carried into their yard. The doe's mother had been killed, and the wobbly little orphan stayed with us for a month while Mom nursed her back to health.

Papa listened quietly to my request and, after checking with Mom, bought me a Daisy air rifle that afternoon. We walked deep into the fields of the farm, and he hung paper targets up on an old fence. We carefully measured twenty steps back, turned, and aimed. I wasn't too bad a shot, but I definitely missed a lot. I got better over time, and he made sure to teach me every safety precaution possible. Learning how to make a precise shot gave me a sense of peace. It made me feel like I was in control, which I needed, because it was becoming increasingly clear to me that something in my life was unbalanced.

That strange feeling was always exacerbated during the holidays, when the distinction between boys and girls becomes much more obvious. When I was five, Mom dressed me as a pink poodle for Halloween. I hated the way I looked in the costume, and I couldn't understand why all the grown-ups were making such a fuss over me. It was basically no different from any of my dance costumes. But the night was saved when I came home from trick-or-treating and spent the rest of the evening playing with an animatronic zombie hand that wiggled and made screaming sounds. Every year after that, I dressed in blood and guts, while the girls around me donned princess gowns and steered clear of me so I wouldn't get gore on their costumes.

Easter was much scarier than Halloween for me. The day before, Mom would always take me to the mall to pick out a new dress to wear to church. For whatever reason, celebrating the resurrection of Jesus goes hand in hand with pastel shades, and those softly hued frocks and matching hair ribbons were murder on my eyes. The one time I was allowed to pick out my own outfit, I chose the simplest, plainest white shift I could find. But even that was too much—I couldn't wait to smear it with grass stains during the egg hunt. Our Easter baskets loudly and proudly reflected the culturally accepted gender norms—pink for girls, blue for boys. Despite my protests I always got stuck with one of the pink baskets, but Gigi would sneak special little gifts into mine, like a pocketknife or a compass.

Christmas became the big yearly reminder that I was different. Take, for example, my letter to Santa from when I was ten:

*Dear Santa Clause, thank you for your presents. Can I
please have a bell off your sleigh? My presents I want are
listed below Merry Christmas!*

> *portabel mattress*
> *backpack*
> *freeze dried food*
> *swiss army pocket knife*
> *pots and pans (camping)*
> *hiking boots*
> *tent that I can hook onto my backpack*
> *air soft gun*
> *camoflodge pants*
> *camoflodge shirt*
> *20 mile range walkie talkies*
> *canteen*
> *hiking stick*
> *anything else that is camping or army or whatever
>   you prefer*

Love Emerald

Come the morning of December 25, I'd tear the wrapping off a box, hoping for something from my wish list, only to find a frilly skirt. I'd flip out, convinced that Santa had gone to the wrong house. I couldn't understand why I was supposed to automatically like anything that was pink, a disgusting color that oozed weakness and frailty. The shockingly bright primary reds and blues that leapt off the boxes of toy trucks, LEGOs, and action figures that Wesley and my male cousins would receive were like magnets to me. Entire colonies of Barbie dolls went untouched over the years. The only time I did try to remove one from the box, I gave up after failing to untangle the plastic ties that bound her arms and legs to the cardboard backing. The restraints were twisted on with a tightness that bordered on the obscene. I shoved the doll back into the carton and headed outside to play, leaving her creepy smile and dead eyes to gaze permanently out of the display cage.

3

Papa and Gigi are religious, but not in any sort of pious, holier-than-thou way. They've been going to the same church since Mom and Susan were kids, and even though I was baptized as a Methodist, my first few years of education were spent at a Catholic school called Monte Cassino that was run by nuns.

Since I come from such a loud and boisterous family, I was fascinated by the nuns' solitary life. One day during recess I asked one of them why they didn't have families of their own.

"We're married to God," she answered.

I thought about this for a minute. If they were already married to God, that meant they didn't have to be married to a *man*. So I decided for a while to become a nun, because that meant I'd never have to marry a man either, something I definitely didn't want to do, even though I enjoyed playing outside with the boys.

I developed my first crush on a girl when I was seven.

Her name was Laurie, and she was athletic and tomboyish like me. We quickly became buddies.

One day our class took a field trip to Big Splash, a local water park that's been open since my parents were kids. Most of the other girls were too scared to climb up the rickety wood tower to the top of the tallest water slide, but Laurie and I couldn't wait to whoosh down. We spent the entire afternoon hitting the pool as hard as we could, seeing who could make the water froth the most, while the rest of the girls prissily tiptoed around in a nearby wading pool, squealing if even the slightest bit of water touched their hair.

At one point Laurie got out of the pool to run to the bathroom. She was wearing a black bathing suit, and I distinctly remember watching her run away and wondering, *Can I marry a girl?* She was the most fun person to be around, and therefore it only made sense to me that she was the kind of person I'd want to marry someday. But I knew somehow it was a question I couldn't ask out loud. It wasn't that I had been consciously exposed to any sort of homophobia at that point in my life; it was just that any other concept besides a man and a woman marrying hadn't been introduced. I felt that my question about being able to marry Laurie was probably as absurd as asking my mom if I could marry one of our pet dogs. It just wasn't done.

That's not to say that I didn't have the occasional mild crush on a boy, but it was only when I found one who could fully match my enthusiasm for all things outdoors—an equal. I remember one little guy named Billy from a few years later who would sometimes come over after school. My family would tease that he was my boyfriend. I'd ignore them and take him down to the rocks behind our house to shoot BB guns.

One day in the middle of target practice, he turned to me and asked, "So, should we kiss?"

"Um, *no*," I said. "Why don't you concentrate a little harder on hitting that center stump?"

We didn't last much longer after that.

I had met Billy at Lincoln Christian School, which my mom transferred me to in the second grade. I was too young to really care where I went, so it didn't have much of an impact on me at first. Lincoln is a nondenominational private kindergarten-through-twelfth-grade institution that costs close to ten thousand dollars a year. They're known for their high graduation rate, sports programs, and excellent state test scores. Mom wasn't a fanatical Christian or anything, but the school was supposed to be one of the best in the area, and Mom wanted the best for me. She worked hard for it too, at the family business Papa and Gigi had started in 1986 called Danco. It makes custom machine parts for oil pumps, and the offices are attached to a warehouse full of industrial machinery that I loved to watch in action. The forklifts were my favorite—I couldn't wait to be old enough to drive one and have all that strength right at my fingertips. Dad worked at Danco too, and he promised he'd have one of the workers teach me how to operate the machines someday. That was the sort of stuff he was great for—Dad was the good-time guy, always ready to play with me and Wes and our cousins. But Mom was the one who was immersed in the real daily grind of raising us and making sure we got a good education. Lincoln Christian School is massive. It looks like it could be a college campus, with different buildings for the elementary and high school kids. The school has its own church that students and their families were required to attend, unless you got a letter from the pastor of another church, saying that you showed up at his or her church regularly. Since sports were so strongly encouraged, I joined the basketball and softball teams and ran track and cross-country. We had Bible study class every day as part of the regular curriculum, and attended chapel on Wednesdays. "Biblical truths" were also incorporated into regular classes such as social studies and English. Almost any historical event that happened would get related back to a specific Bible quote, and while the teachers didn't shy away from real literature in English classes as I got older, any book that contained a swear had the word meticulously blacked out with a Sharpie in each and every copy.

Lincoln was required by law to teach us Darwin's theory of evolution, but the teachers made sure that we knew it was against their will. Any talk of apes evolving into men was accompanied by huge eye rolls and constant reminders that it was just an idea some people had. But they knew the actual truth—it was Adam and Eve all the way. One teacher even expressed his disdain for evolution through the utterly bizarre comparison of placing a bunch of paper clips inside a small box and telling us, "These aren't going to turn into a rocket ship inside here just because some scientist says so. So how can monkeys turn into men?"

Even though that specific argument didn't quite compute

with me, I was young enough back then to follow the school's doctrines without much questioning. I dutifully memorized Bible passages and believed wholeheartedly in the teachers' version of the gospel. The basic tenets about love and the importance of family resonated strongly.

The school uniform was a gray, black, and maroon plaid skirt with a matching maroon polo shirt. In a way the outfit was a relief. It meant that I didn't have to think about dressing myself, because shopping for clothes was a nightmare. Mom would drag me through the girls' department, loading her arms up with dresses, while I'd stare longingly across the aisle at the boy stuff. It was all just so much more *practical*. If I hadn't already had an assigned school getup, I know that Mom would have insisted I wear things that were ultra-feminine. As it was, she still stuck a bow in my hair every morning before I left the house.

I'd like to say I was a rebel and tore it off right after she dropped me at school, but I didn't. I hated the accessories, but I also couldn't cross Mom. Not because I was scared of what she might do, but because . . . well, she was my mom. It didn't even *occur* to me that I could disobey her. I kept the bows in to make her happy, even though every ribbon felt like a ten-pound rock on my head. My hair was long, and I begged her throughout my entire childhood to let me cut it short, but she'd never let me. I was very aware of the fact that she loved having a little girl, and the pressure to keep up that appearance for her began to take a toll. I became unable to sleep at night, a common symptom of anxiety. It got harder and harder for me to concentrate in class, and I was diagnosed with ADHD and put on medication. But I never made the connection between these mental problems and my confusion about why I felt so different—a sensation that increased more and more each year.

On the school playground, I couldn't understand why teachers discouraged me from playing with boys and insisted I hang with the girls. They made me feel like I was doing something bad. It made me feel like an "other"—an interloper. I lived in some weird dimension, peering out at the rest of existence from the strange prison of a body that didn't match my mind. I knew that the church community had expectations of me because of how *they* defined me, but I wanted to define myself. And trying to do that was complicated. It wasn't like I'd thought, *Oh, I'm actually a guy* from the get-go; that concept didn't exist in my world yet. I didn't even know you were *allowed* to think like that. Still, I tried to assert myself in little ways that came naturally to me. For example, when I'd meet someone new, I'd say, "Hi, I'm Emerald," in the deepest growl I could muster, because the voice that came out of my mouth on its own wasn't the one that I heard inside my head.

One weekend during the fourth grade, I spent the night at a cousin's house from my dad's side of the family, a guy named Tye who is the same age as me. I had an annual mile run for gym class the next day, but I'd forgotten to bring any running clothes. So he let me borrow some of his—a black, skintight tank top and black shorts. I slipped them on and immediately felt a rush of power, like I'd put on a superhero suit. They were so easy and simple—there were no hidden zippers to mess with, tiny buttons to fasten, or collars to smooth down.

The next day I ran the mile and made my best time ever up to that point. Tye let me keep the shorts and shirt, and I'd change into them the second I got home from school. Whenever I went to visit Tye after that, I would ask to try on more of his clothes, and he'd let me take additional pieces home. Mom didn't really mind—she thought I was doing it because I looked up to him.

But while I was happy to have my own growing collection of boys' clothes, one thing continued to frustrate me. When I'd put on a pair of shorts or jeans, they'd fold inward between my legs. And I knew that they weren't supposed to look like that. There was supposed to be a bulge there.

I knew exactly what that missing shape was, despite the fact that no one had ever sat me down and recited the old "birds and the bees" speech. Mom gave me a book at one point that I promptly hid behind my dresser out of embarrassment, and the health teachers at Lincoln might as well have been walking and talking genital-free dolls, for the amount of information they had to offer. But I did have one valuable resource. When you have as many cousins as I do, you absorb a *lot* of knowledge. I picked up bits and pieces about bodies and what you could do with them, and it all seemed gross but sort of thrilling, mainly because it was something that no one else was talking about. It was secret information, handed down from cousin to cousin, full of half-truths, outright myths, and penis jokes. And it was the penis stuff that fascinated me the most.

I saw a lot of penises as a little kid. Group baths, getting the mud showered off us after a day at the farm, and swimming were all normal cousin activities. None of us were taught to have shame about our bodies, yet I still felt it. I wished I could stand up and just pee wherever I wanted when we were playing outside, like my cousin Dewayne did. I'd seethe with jealousy whenever I had to run inside or hide behind a bush, while he could just let it fly.

One day when I was alone in my room messing around with blue Play-Doh, I rolled some quickly between my hands to make a snake. The shape started to take on another familiar form. I stuck a round ball on the tip and walked up to the mirror, holding it between my legs. *That's more like it,* I thought.

I began experimenting with ways to pee standing up. I soaked my thighs a lot in the beginning, but after a while I developed a method of hiking one leg up against a tree and then straining really hard to force the stream out with more precision. This worked maybe 50 percent of the time.

I had a lot of magazines on camping and outdoor life that I'd beg Mom to buy me at the grocery store. I started to notice ads in the back for funnel devices that allowed women to pee standing up, but I knew instinctively that I couldn't ask Mom to get one for me. All of my outdoor bathroom experiments took place alone. I was embarrassed—not because I was trying to pee like a boy but because I couldn't do it on my own. It just seemed like something I should already be able to do.

I finally snuck on to Mom's computer and searched "how to pee standing up." And I learned how to craft a homemade funnel. It involved a plastic canister lid, so I watched Mom like a hawk every morning when she made coffee, and monitored the level of grounds inside the container whenever she wasn't looking. I had to wait about a week, but I finally caught her throwing the can into the recycling bin.

I snuck into the garage, removed the lid, and carefully trimmed off the lip with a pair of scissors, until it was just a simple, flexible round disc. I drank three huge glasses of water and waited until I had to go, and then ran out into the woods. I pulled down my pants, rolled the lid into a cone shape, and let my bladder go. It worked! I went back inside and cleaned the disc off. From that day on, I wouldn't leave the house without it whenever I went to play outside. But I kept it a secret. I'd still go behind a bush if my cousins were around. I was proud of my newfound skill, but I knew that I would get teased if I showed anyone what I'd learned. Although camping magazines let me know that other girls were doing the same thing I was, the very fact that the ads were tucked away in the back of the issues let me know it was something to keep hidden.

I had one close friend who had body issues too, but for an entirely different reason. Her name was Andi; she was hard-core Baptist and incredibly modest. Like, Amish modest. She hated to show any skin below the collarbone, and would even sit on her hands whenever she was finished eating a meal. Like me, she hated wearing a bathing suit when we'd go swimming, and would instead put on shorts and a T-shirt.

Andi didn't go to Lincoln—we had met in dance class,

and by fourth grade we were both focused solely on clogging. Luckily the costumes were very reserved. Since Andi was as shy about her body as I was about mine, we'd sneak off together to the bathroom and change into our outfits while locked safely inside the stalls. Our team was coed, and we usually all wore the same version of what was basically a glorified tracksuit. We'd clog our brains out in purple, white, and navy outfits, but to modern songs such as "Let It Rock." I genuinely liked the dancing, but I felt uncomfortable in front of the crowds. I was very aware that my long hair was flying everywhere, just like all the other girls'. I'd lose focus, staring with jealousy at the boys' streamlined bodies, all the straight lines of their torsos, and hair so short that it did exactly what they wanted it to do. They just looked *cleaner* somehow.

For my birthday in fourth grade, Mom invited Andi and all the girls on my school's basketball team over. She dumped a huge pile of makeup onto the dining room table and said, "Have at it!"

Everyone squealed and dove their little hands into the sea of pink and red lipsticks. Compacts of blush skittered around the table like hockey pucks, and the air was quickly filled with the harsh, chemical pinch of nail polish. Andi and I took one look at each other and marched outside to play secret agents. I had a bunch of little toy tools, like a flashlight that transformed into a periscope, and we took turns spying on the girls through the window, with a mix of awe and disgust. Neither of us could understand the allure of smearing those garish colors all over our faces.

Another big part of what I loved about Andi was that she

had this weird, offbeat personality. She was constantly sending me these bizarre, imaginary missions via e-mail. Things like:

Go to the electrical outlet located in your bedroom, the one that's just to the left of your chinchilla cage. Knock on it three times, and a secret door will open up next to it. Enter the tunnel and crawl forward until you reach a crossroad. There you will find a red button. After you press the button, a small troll will appear. Recite the alphabet backward to him, and when you get to the letter T, he will call a tiny zebra to give you a ride to your next task.

I'd pretend to do whatever it was that she told me, and then I'd send her back instructions of my own, so that even when we were apart, we could continue running rampant through our imaginations together.

Mom ended up becoming good friends with Andi's mother, Kelli. Our families would caravan on trips, like to the Crater of Diamonds State Park in Arkansas, where our pretend adventures could actually come true because we'd get to go on digs for actual gems. We never found any, but that wasn't the point. The fact that our mothers indulged and encouraged these fantasies was its own sort of treasure.

On one overnight camping excursion, our mothers rented a small cabin by a lake. Andi and I went exploring along the shoreline and came upon a giant piece of Styrofoam, bigger than a twin-size mattress. We both had the same idea immediately—boat! We went into the woods and collected branches that we fashioned into oars, and then we pushed out into the water. We cruised along the shoreline all afternoon, captains of our own private world.

As awesome as my friendship with Andi was, Mom was worried that I didn't have anyone from Lincoln to hang out with, since Andi and my cousins attended different schools. The girls from my basketball team were okay, but my mom's attempt to have me forge new bonds with them at the makeup birthday party had failed because of my disinterest in the theme, and Billy had stopped talking to me after I'd refused to kiss him. It wasn't like I didn't *want* other friends, but I felt so separate from almost everyone else that I had no idea how to even approach people. I always sat alone at lunch.

The one girl from Lincoln who lived in our neighborhood was named Heather, and she was a classic popular mean girl. She ignored me completely whenever she saw me on the street, and in school she constantly made fun of me to my face about the masculine way I walked and talked. She'd imitate my awkward shuffle down the hallway, and repeat anything I said in a mocking, cartoonish low voice.

Her best friend was a girl named Jillian who was on my basketball team. In fourth grade Jillian and Heather were in different classes. Jillian ended up in mine, and I was surprised to discover that she was actually a pretty nice person. Maybe being separated from Heather's influence did her some good, because one day, out of the blue, she invited me to sit with her at the pizza joint our basketball team always went to after a game. From that point forward she sat with me at lunch every day. She did most of the talking—mostly about who liked whom in our school—but she didn't seem to mind or care that I didn't say much in return. I didn't care about the gossip; I was just happy to no longer be eating alone.

Lincoln is such a huge school that the cafeteria is located in a separate building far away from the main campus, in a giant structure that also serves as the mega church that most of the kids at our school went to. We'd file on to buses to get driven there and back from the classroom buildings.

One Friday, Mom showed up at the cafeteria and sat down with Jillian and me.

"Would you like to have a sleepover with Emerald tonight?" she asked Jillian.

I was secretly grateful. I wanted to hang out with Jillian more since she was being so nice, but I was so socially awkward that I had no idea how to further the friendship.

"I'd love to," she said. "Somehow I just knew that you were going to ask me that! I'll call my dad and see if he'll bring a bag for me after school."

He agreed, and Mom was determined to make it a special night, one that forced lots of social interaction. She didn't want us to just sit around and watch movies, since she was trying to get me out of my shell.

She took us to a fondue restaurant, and then out for shakes, and when we got back to the house, she offered to let us take a bubble bath in her giant Jacuzzi tub.

"Oh, yes!" Jillian squealed.

"No," I said firmly.

"You won't be *naked*," Mom said. "Jillian can borrow a bathing suit."

I certainly had enough unused ones in my dresser, but

I still said no. The thought of getting into a tub with this girl horrified me. Even if I wore my standard shorts and T-shirt, it was just still too close and intimate. It filled me with dread. In such slippery, small quarters I didn't want her to see *any* part of my body that was normally covered by clothing. Mom and Jillian begged and pleaded for me to relent, but I refused.

Mom finally gave up and put on a movie for us to watch. I snuck off into the kitchen and tugged on her shirt.

"Mom, where is she going to *sleep*?" I asked.

"In your bed," she said, looking surprised. "It's big. There's room for two."

"No way," I said. "Nope."

"What are you talking about?" she whispered so Jillian couldn't hear in the other room. "That's what little girls do! You sleep in the same bed, and you can even stay up late if you want and talk!"

"Uh-uh," I said, shaking my head.

She got frustrated. "Where is she going to sleep, then? We can't put her on the couch!"

I brightened. "Cool. Then *I'll* sleep on the couch. She can have my room to herself!"

Mom wasn't having that. I finally gave in and agreed to sleep in the bed with her, but I stayed close enough to the edge that I ran the risk of tumbling out in my sleep. Except that I *couldn't* sleep. I just stared for hours at the outline of my bedside lamp in the dark. It was shaped like a poodle, with a white lamp shade surrounded by fluffy pink trim. (Mom had decorated my room; *everything* was pink.)

I tried to figure out what my feelings meant. I didn't want my friend to have any proximity to my body, or me to hers. Maybe it was because their similarities only compounded my confusion about what I felt was wrong with mine. And even though I was fully clothed in pajamas, the thin material hardly acted as a sufficient barrier. The whole situation was just too awkward.

Looking back, it's funny to think that just a few years later I'd be longing for the days when Mom was willing to toss me under the sheets with a girl and close the door.

Jillian's father came and got her in the morning, and later that day I was playing soldier in the yard by myself when I felt someone standing nearby. I glanced up and saw Heather looming over me, scowling.

"You are not allowed to be friends with Jillian," she snarled. "She is MY friend."

"Whatever, Heather," I mumbled.

"I mean it," she said threateningly.

Heather must have said something to Jillian, because Jillian avoided me from then on. Mom made one last attempt at finding me friends at school by inviting *all* the girls on my basketball team over for a sleepover. Their mothers must have insisted they attend; it was the only reason I could think of as to why they'd show up. Normally I hardly spoke to any of them unless we were on the court.

On the night of the slumber party, I essentially became a stranger in my own home. At one point all the girls herded themselves into the bathroom to play with their hair, and I wandered in to try to integrate.

"What's up, guys?" I said.

Jillian turned to me, narrowing her eyes into mean little slits. "What are you doing in here?" she said. "Get out!"

I didn't even bother trying to sleep in the same room with them that night. Everyone piled up together in our den, but I unrolled my camo sleeping bag in the living room and tossed and turned with a pillow pressed over my ears in an attempt to drown out the giggles and high-pitched squeals coming from the other room.

At least I have Andi, I consoled myself as I finally managed to drift off. I wished she could have been there to help make the night bearable. I believed with all my heart that she would be my best friend for life. I was totally clueless that she'd soon turn her back on me, just like Jillian had.

4

Sometime just after the start of fifth grade, Mom picked me up from school as usual, but out of nowhere she started talking about how I was going to grow breasts someday. I was horrified. I had been so preoccupied with what I *didn't* have on my body that it hadn't even occurred to me what I *would* have.

But it got worse.

Once we got back to the house, she took me into my bedroom. I stared at the wall as Mom explained that in addition to breasts, I was going to start my cycle. She did a good job of giving me all the biological reasons why it was going to happen and why it was natural and normal, but I was stuck on one detail. Blood was going to come out of my vagina.

Somehow this part of the female body experience hadn't been covered by my cousins' sex talks.

"Will it hurt?" I asked.

"No, but sometimes when it happens you'll get a tummy ache. Not every time, though."

My jaw dropped.

"What do you mean, *every* time?" I asked.

"Oh, no, honey," she said. "I'm sorry if you misunderstood. It's not just a onetime thing. Once it starts, it will happen every month for most of your life."

I burst into tears. No matter how much she tried to assure me that it would mean I was becoming a woman, and that it happened to everyone and was perfectly normal, I kept crying. Blood pouring out of your body was not natural as far as I was concerned. *Especially* down there. And if it was something that was supposed to happen to girls, then it definitely wasn't supposed to happen to me. But I was still too young to even know what that thought actually meant. It wasn't that I *hated* having a vagina. I just wanted a penis. With the exception of the peeing-while-standing issue, it had been pretty easy up until that point to pretend that my vagina just wasn't there. But now that I knew what it had in store for me, I wanted nothing to do with it.

It turned out that Mom had been right on time with her talk about boobs, because not long after, I woke up with a sore chest. It started as a weird achy feeling, like I'd been hit really hard by a basketball at practice. Soon after that I noticed that small knots were forming under my nipples, and they began to protrude. I'd hold my hands over them every night, lying on my stomach, trying to keep them flattened. It didn't work. The sides began to fill up and out as well, and before I knew it, there they were. Two bumps that looked like a weird set of googly eyes staring back at me from the mirror whenever I got out of the shower. I'd cover them with a towel as fast as possible.

I realized that if I hunched over, I could make them disappear somewhat into my shirt. I started to walk with my shoulders forward, which only increased my boyish stomp. I refused to wear a bra. I couldn't even say the word, it felt so embarrassing on my tongue. There was no way in hell I was going to have one of those things touching my skin. It was bad enough that I was forced to wear things like skirts and bows on the outside—wearing a bra hidden under my shirt, pressed tight against my skin, felt like a betrayal to myself, like admitting defeat. And I wasn't ready to do that yet. I was in such denial about my chest that I'd wear loose tank tops at home, totally oblivious to the fact that my breasts would pop out the sides whenever I'd climb a tree. Red-carpet celebrity nip slips have nothing on what I was unintentionally flashing that year.

The girls at school all started to develop around the same time as well. Unlike me, they were psyched about it. The bold ones would pull their shirts down over their shoulders when the teachers weren't looking, to show off their newest bra colors to their friends. The more subtle way of announcing to the class that you were finally wearing a bra was to pull your shirt tight against your back while sitting in class, so that everyone could see the strap outline through the cloth. I would defiantly pull my polo tight too, to show everyone that I *wasn't* wearing a bra. I was asserting myself, desperate to stay as physically separate from the girls as possible.

It started to get really bad in basketball. I couldn't hunch when I ran, and so my breasts would flop up and down like small water balloons. The girls on the team started to make snide comments, and after one particularly aggressive game, Mom came up to me afterward and said, "That's it. I'm getting you some bras."

The next day I was sitting on the couch watching television with my cousin Tye when Mom came home from Target. She held up one of the bags, and as if in slow motion, I saw her mouth start to open. I realized with horror that she was about to announce that she'd bought me some bras, and I refused to allow Tye—the provider of all my boy clothes—to know that I was about to become the owner of a bra.

I leapt up from the couch and reached her just as she started to say, "I got you . . ."

I tore the bag from her hand and saw that there was a box of candy canes on top of the pile of cloth. I yanked them out and held them high.

"Candy canes!" I yelled, finishing her sentence for her. "Thanks, Mom. I love candy canes!"

I tore upstairs as fast as I could and sat down on my bed, tossing the candy aside. I pulled one of the bras out of the bag. It was white, with pink piping that ran the circumference of each cup. Mom appeared in my doorway, and I held the offending garment up to her.

"This is *hideous*," I said.

"Well, no one has to see it, now, do they?" she said.

"*I* have to," I muttered.

From that point on we compromised on black sports bras, which at least managed to flatten my chest some. But it was a small consolation.

The only thing that managed to cheer me up those days was motocross. I'd gotten my first dirt bike when I was eight, a blue TT R 90 Yamaha, and Dad had helped me clear trails back behind our house for me to ride on. My asthma had continued to get worse, making basketball and track harder and harder. The combo of physical exercise and being out-doors would trigger awful attacks. But on my bike I could travel faster than I could run, with none of the same physical exertion that triggered my lungs. What I had loved so much about running was the feeling of flying, of leaving myself behind as I pushed farther ahead. Motocross not only moved me more quickly away from the starting line, but I caught air whenever I rode over a hill. For split seconds at a time I could feel myself above the ground. Some people take drugs or drink in order to get out of themselves, to forget their lives—for me the exhilaration of leaving the earth's surface gave me the same sensation. All of my bodily discomfort, all my insecurity, all my anxiety, would disappear. It would just be me, alone in the air, weightless, even if for just a tiny instant.

But those moments were too few and far between. In addi-tion to school, sports, and dance, Mom decided to tack on yet another activity. Pretty much everyone—Mom, Dad, Susan, my grandparents—began to notice how uncomfortable I was getting onstage during my dance performances. They couldn't understand why I was so active and social at home with my family but withdrawn and shy when out in public. Mom kept trying to build me up, telling me how pretty I was, not realizing that it was exactly the *wrong* thing to say to me.

And so she had the brilliant idea to enter me into the confidence-boosting world of child beauty pageants.

Her reasoning was that if I could finally see how pretty I was—and have a bunch of *other* people also tell me how pretty I was—I'd start to feel better about myself. I sometimes wonder, though, if she was also subconsciously trying to fix my rejection of femininity. It's the only other reason I can think of as to why she'd enroll me into such a hyper-girly environment, the antithesis of everything I liked. I went along with it because I didn't want to disappoint her.

Mom started staying up late, searching eBay for pageant dresses in my size, and in colors that made me want to vomit. Everything had some element of sparkly sequins built into it, designed to glimmer onstage. Aunt Susan got in on the action too, and decided to enroll her youngest daughter, Diamond, in the pageants as well.

(I know, I know. Emerald and Diamond. It was a coincidence, though—Diamond had already been given her name when Susan adopted her.)

At first the pageants were a disaster. Mom would put old-fashioned sponge curlers in my hair the night before so I'd have these perfect, cascading ringlets, but the cylinders hurt me so much, and I complained so loudly, that she eventually started waiting until I had fallen asleep before coming into my room and rolling my hair while I was unconscious.

We had to travel out of town for a lot of events, so we'd pack all the equipment into the car at dawn, and I'd be exhausted and out of it by the time we arrived at whatever hotel ballroom we were competing in. I'd change into my dress in a bathroom stall, away from the other girls, and Mom would wait until the very last minute to put my makeup on. Lipstick was the worst—that greasy, caked-on layer of lurid red over my mouth felt so heavy. Smiling was an exercise in torture, and if you've ever seen a pageant, you know that the smile is everything.

Well, that and your walk. And I could not walk. I'd stomp out onstage and lumber from one end to the other, then head back toward center stage, where I'd plant my feet shoulder-width apart. I was so bad at it that Mom paid for lessons, like those runway classes that they do on *America's Next Top Model.*

After I'd complete the walk, the judges would ask questions about what I liked to do in my free time.

"Motocross and play army," I'd always say, trying to force the corners of my lips up in a gross facsimile of a smile.

Some judges would like the response, since it set me apart from the other girls, but others would mark points off for it. But the one part of the ceremony that I always excelled at was the talent segment. Even though I wasn't as good a dancer as the girls in my regular classes back home, I'd still been doing it for almost my whole life. I would get into the competitive spirit and blow the other contestants at the pageants out of the water. Some girl would sing a horrible, off-key rendition of "The Star-Spangled Banner," and then I'd walk out onstage and clog so fast that my feet were a blur. And thanks to that skill, I started earning trophies—ridiculously tall columns topped with gold statues of girls in dresses holding scepters. Mom still has them all, hidden away in a spare room in our house, along with a closet stuffed with all my dresses.

Everyone told me how beautiful I looked in the clown makeup, and while I didn't believe it for a second, getting any sort of positive reinforcement felt good, since I was starting to be bullied even harder at school for being too masculine. Girls would yell out at me to stay away from their stall when I entered the bathroom, as if I were some perv trying to spy on them, and Heather's taunts about the way I walked down the hallway continued.

My single attempt to appease the girls at school backfired, hard. One weekend after getting my hair trimmed for a pageant, I decided to actually try to make it look nice for school, too. I parted it in a different way that definitely made me look more feminine. It was a style that I knew a pageant judge would appreciate, and I hoped that maybe it would make a difference outside of that small world.

Monday morning as I got to my locker, I heard a girl call out my name. I turned around and saw one of Heather's friends, a girl named Erica. She was staring at my hair, and I felt my hopes rise.

"Nice haircut," she sneered, and then laughed in my face. I blushed and turned back to my locker to open it and put my books away, and she suddenly kneed me in the tailbone. My chin smashed against the metal locker, and my books spilled all over the floor. It *hurt*. I heard everyone around us laugh and then scatter as the bell rang. I gathered my stuff off the ground, refusing to cry.

I couldn't win on Lincoln's turf, so in a way, Mom was

right about the pageant circuit boosting my ego a little—I'd drink up kind words however I could get them. But whenever I looked in the mirror before going onstage, I still had no idea who the painted harlequin was looking back at me.

In addition to talent, I started winning trophies for things like Most Photogenic. In real life my actions and movements were totally butch. I'd storm out onto a stage in a yellow bathing suit with clear heels, and stand with my legs spread like a bull rider, while every other little girl kept their legs demurely crossed. But frozen in a picture, with glossy hair, a body-hugging dress, limbs posed by Mom, and a fake smile that hid everything I felt inside, the illusion worked. It was the ultimate in false reality.

As the pageants dragged on, I also got better and better at motocross. Not only were the races exhilarating, but I'd get to suit up in full-body protective gear that hid my breasts, and a helmet that hid my hair. You know those moments in an action movie when a stranger screeches to a halt on a motorcycle, and you think it's a dude, but then the person takes off the helmet, and as long hair comes pouring out while the head shakes back and forth in slow motion, you realize it's a lady? Well, I never wanted to take the helmet off.

I ended up winning the talent portion of the Oklahoma state championship pageant for my expert clogging to "Cotton-Eyed Joe." But when the judges found out that I wouldn't be able to make it to nationals because that pageant overlapped with a gig my dance studio had booked for us on a cruise line, they decided to strip me of my title.

"We need to give it to the first runner-up so that we

have someone to represent Oklahoma," they told Mom. She wasn't having it, and only returned the sash, keeping the trophy and crown for our collection.

"We already paid for them," she said, fuming. She was right—the entry fees were expensive, and the cost of those prizes came right out of her pocket.

She was so annoyed about the situation that we ended up quitting pageants for good after that. The whole experience was pretty absurd, but there is one title that I am still proud to have won, one with a name that pretty much sums up how I felt about myself at the time: At a competition in my hometown, I had been crowned Miss Broken Arrow.

5

I woke up one morning in seventh grade to the sound of rain hitting the roof. I rolled over and stared out the window for a while before getting out of bed. There wasn't any sort of wind whipping the trees around to make the weather look cool or dramatic—just a steady, determined downfall, the kind of rain that makes you want to crawl as deep under your covers as possible and disappear.

I managed to drag myself from bed, avoiding all mirrors, even though my body was safely shrouded in plaid pajama pants and a faded Def Leppard T-shirt. I felt off. Not exactly sick, but a strange depression seemed to be pulling at my feet, and my brain was a fog. Not even my new bedroom on our house's second floor, with its walls stripped bare of anything pink, could cheer me up.

I showered, numb as usual to my breasts, aware of them only as objects, something external to run soap over. I closed my eyes, let the water pour over me, but all I could see in my head was the water coming from the sky outside, gray droplets soaking me and making my long hair stick to my back, weighing me down.

I gathered my hair all into a ponytail at the back of my head and pulled tight. The skin of my skull stretched until it stung, and for the millionth time I imagined rushing out, grabbing the scissors from my desk, and slicing through the thick rope I'd formed. I could hear the sound it would make, the thrilling, satisfying crunch of a thousand tiny strands splintering until I was free. I pulled the hair up and over my head and twisted it harder into a knot, pretending for a minute that it was all gone. The shower water now ran freely down my naked back, and for a moment I felt truly clean.

I dried off and pulled on my uniform before heading downstairs. My plaid skirt was rumpled and smelled off, like musty day-old socks. I noticed a small stain near the hem but shrugged it off.

My brother, Wesley, was at the kitchen table still half-asleep, listlessly shoveling Reese's Puffs cereal into his mouth. You'd think the sugar would jolt him out of his stupor, but it didn't seem to have any effect. The smell of bacon, fried eggs, and toast, normally so comforting, just made me feel slightly nauseous and did nothing to cut through the gloom outside.

By the time I got to school, the rain was coming down harder. I drifted from class to class in a haze. After fourth period I stopped in the bathroom before heading to lunch. I refused to make eye contact with anyone as I slunk down to the stall at the far end, away from the row of sinks and chicks fixing their hair in the mirrors. I shut the door, locked it, and collapsed down onto the toilet, grateful to be out of sight.

I let the weight of my head pull my gaze down toward my ankles as I peed.

There was blood in my underwear.

Not a lot, just a few spots, but enough for me to know that it was finally happening. This final injustice, a giant middle finger to my mind from inside my body. The red stains seemed like they were mocking me.

You can't do anything to stop us, they sneered. *And there's a whole lot more where we came from.*

The walls of the stall started to close in around me, and an asthma attack began to creep in. I felt betrayed. I wanted to rip the pair of underwear off and throw away this proof of the inevitable, but that was impossible—I was trapped in every way imaginable. Four walls around me, and a body that was determined to morph into something I had no mental connection to.

I started to panic. What if more blood suddenly started pouring out of me any minute now? I'd have rather died than call out and ask a stranger for a pad. I wadded up a bunch of toilet paper and stuffed it into my underwear in case anything else came out. I stood up and bunched it all into place so nothing seemed bulky or weird underneath my skirt. I flushed, took a huge breath, and walked out of the stall. Thankfully, most of the girls were gone by then. I washed my hands and fled to my locker to get my phone. On the bus ride up to the cafeteria, I shot my Mom an urgent text.

Come get me now.

She wrote back a few minutes later. *What's wrong?*

Just come. Please.

• • •

When the bus dropped us back at the school after lunch, I saw her car parked in front. I broke from the rest of the kids heading inside and ran through the rain and climbed in. Mom stared at me with a funny look on her face.

"Did you start?" she asked.

I nodded and stared down at my lap. I was happy for the small favor that she had somehow sensed the problem, because I couldn't even say the words "I got my period." It was like the trap of my body had sealed my mouth shut too.

"We can go get you some things," she said.

We stopped at Danco to pick up Susan before heading to Drug Warehouse. My aunt could sense the mood as soon as she got into the car. "It's doomsday!" she said, and cackled, massaging my shoulder. "Oh, honey, I hate it too. It's a bloody mess." I managed a weak smile.

When we got to the store, I followed them glumly to the "feminine needs" aisle. I stood at the end. I couldn't bring myself to walk down it.

"Do you want tampons?" Mom asked, a little too loudly.

"Ugh, no!" Susan yelled. "I never stick those things in me!"

"Keep your voice down," I hissed, ducking into the aisle and grabbing the nearest box of pads I could reach and tossing it into the basket. "Let's go."

We drove back to Danco, and they ushered me into the conference room.

"It's really easy to put on," Mom explained, pulling a pad out of the box.

Susan grabbed it from her hands. "Look at the wings!" she said, making them flap up and down, trying to get me to smile again.

It didn't work that time.

The next morning I woke up doubled over in cramps. I begged Mom to let me stay home from school, but she wasn't having it. I was still just spotting, but after my first class I felt this awful leaking sensation between my legs. I tried squeezing like when you have to pee, but it did nothing. I ran to the bathroom, stopping at my locker to grab a hoodie, along with a fresh pad that I slipped inside the sleeve so that no one would notice.

I got to the bathroom, and there was so much blood. More than I could have imagined. I grimly cleaned up, changed my pad, and headed back to class. An hour later the same leaking feeling started again, and I headed back to the bathroom. It went on like clockwork, every hour for the rest of the day.

I wanted to die.

Over the next few months I kept up the same system as that first day for grabbing pads when needed. Since I was the only girl in school who didn't carry a purse, I'd keep them hidden in my backpack until I needed to head to the bathroom. I'd slip one inside the sleeve of a hoodie before going to the bathroom, and once I was safely inside a stall, I'd open up the pad as slowly and silently as possible. I'd put the used one inside the little metal box on the wall, but made sure to close the lid ever so gently so it wouldn't make its telltale slamming sound and announce to everyone in the room that I had my period.

But while I could hide what was happening from the people around me, I was now directly confronted on a monthly basis with the reality of my body. My breasts, hips, and long hair—I'd developed ways to try to block them from my mind, and to hide all the physical traits the best I could with baggy clothes and a hat. Even my pubic hair helped block the sight of my vagina.

But blood is undeniable. As was the shame it caused. My period was an affront. And my fury about the indignity and unfairness of it caused me to sink more deeply into depression. Tampon commercials on television sent me into a rage. Those perfectly coiffed women in their soft-hued cardigans and summer dresses were supposed to make me feel a sense of camaraderie with womankind. The promise in those ads is that *We're all in this together.* But every time my period started, I felt further and further apart from the rest of the world.

I still had motocross to keep me distracted, along with Papa and Gigi's farm and our huge, forested backyard, with its boulders and dense trees. I was old enough to start building fires outside by myself. My favorite spot to build them was on the giant rocks, and one afternoon when I was down there, I noticed that a space between two of them would make a perfect little cave if it had a cover.

I had started skateboarding around this time too, and one of Mom's friends had helped me build a half-pipe in the garage for me and Wes. There was some wood left over from the construction, so I covered the gap between the boulders and piled leaves and twigs and moss on top. It became my hideout from the world. A place I could escape to and absorb the nature around me. For all the religion I was faced with at Lincoln, I was starting to realize that I felt much more spiritual when I was in the woods or any other sort of natural surrounding. The feel of bark against my cheek while I was up in a tree gave me more peace than scripture ever did. It was becoming increasingly harder for me to ignore the hypocrisy of the students at my school—they claimed to be Christians, but it was in image only. The fact that they could quote the Bible and showed up at church every Sunday didn't prevent them from being relentlessly cruel. And I knew strongly in my heart that true Christians shouldn't persecute someone for being different—it goes against all the most basic tenets of the religion, the ones like love, tolerance, and charity.

I was practicing that last one in earnest by volunteering at an animal sanctuary located in Broken Arrow. It's home to hundreds of rescued exotic pets from all over the country—peacocks, monkeys, tigers, wolves, kangaroos, and even a hybrid liger named Rocky. I'd get up at seven a.m. every Saturday and Sunday to help out. Since I was a junior volunteer, my chores mostly included shoveling crap, but I also got to feed the birds of prey. You had to work there for several years before you were allowed to interact with any of the larger animals. I didn't care if all I was doing was minor chores, though; being able to help these creatures out in any way I could made me happy. I understood them— born who they were but trapped by circumstance.

One morning the older volunteers let me ride in the back of their pickup with them down to the big cat cages to help feed the liger. Technically this was against the rules. I wasn't allowed anywhere near that part of the sanctuary, so I stayed in the truck bed and helped them chop up raw meat. The workers hooked chunks of flesh onto a large metal pole and stuck it over the fence and into the pen. Rocky leapt up for it, propelling himself what looked like six feet off the ground to get what he needed to survive.

It reminded me of my own small flights from the earth when I was on my dirt bike. I needed those moments suspended in the air for my sanity, in the same way that the liger needed to leave the ground to catch his food, the very thing that kept him alive.

That afternoon Dad took me off-roading in his Bronco. We flew across fields that stretched out forever, and laughed when our heads knocked the ceiling after crazy bumps. He pulled over as we neared the edge of a giant quarry, and we walked to the edge to investigate. It looked as if aliens had come and taken a mile-wide scoop out of the earth, exposing steep cliffs that plummeted down into still water. We sat near the edge, absorbing the silence.

"Your mom and I are getting a divorce," he suddenly said.

I let that sink in for minute, but I can't say that I was surprised. He and Mom hadn't exactly been spending a lot of time together. He'd come home from work and disappear into their bedroom and watch television while she cooked us dinner and helped us with our homework.

"We still love each other and are still friends, but I'm going to be moving out," he said.

"Okay," I answered. I didn't really know how to respond. I think at the time, more than anything else, I was just pissed that he'd ruined such an awesome afternoon. But I knew that he was loyal to us and wouldn't disappear from our lives. I was right—he ended up moving into a place in nearby Catoosa, and in my mind I got to become the man of the house I'd always pictured myself as anyway. Nothing about the divorce was traumatic—Dad still worked with Mom at Danco, and they actually started getting along much better, becoming the friends that they were way more cut out to be for each other.

And lucky for me, his new home would soon provide a much needed haven from my mother's wrath over my first real love—the appropriately surnamed Darian Storms.

I'd been noticing Darian around the dance studio since I was twelve but didn't really meet her until I was thirteen and had graduated into the mid-range group at Moore's Dance Studio—the Electric Shock team. Darian was two years older than me and in the top-tier group, Shockwave. My practice sessions started a full hour earlier than hers, but our practices overlapped by thirty minutes, so that we could watch her and the rest of the older kids dance and try to pick up some of their fancier steps. But a lot of the time Darian was already at the studio by the time I arrived, since she also helped out the teachers with the much younger kids, whose classes started even earlier.

Darian was shorter than me, with long straight red hair, green eyes, some freckles splashed across her cheeks, and ginormous boobs. Like, so big that she sometimes had to strap them down with an Ace bandage when she danced if it required particularly vigorous moves—not even a sports bra would cut it.

Every year Moore's participated in the Tulsa Downtown Parade of Lights, a huge holiday celebration full of floats sponsored by local businesses. It's a two-and-a-half-mile-long gig, and we'd dance every step of the way in short-skirted Santa outfits, no matter how cold it was. Despite the stupid costume, I actually enjoyed it—I viewed it as a test of my endurance, since you have to be in pretty sick shape to dance for that long without stopping. But that year I was having trouble learning the steps. The song was "Toy Soldier" by Britney Spears, and it required some pretty complex footwork. Imagine someone barking "hop double double heel step step touch up heel up hop double back hop double hop double pull back" at you for hours on end, and you get a sense of what I was up against. It was like that movie *Happy Feet* on crack.

One of the teachers asked Darian to help me learn the dance. Darian practiced with my cousins Cheyenne and Amanda and me until we all had the steps down.

On the day of the parade, Darian and I were hanging out on some sound equipment when she suddenly asked for my phone number. I gave it to her, and we started texting back and forth. She teased me constantly about the fact that I believed in God and went to a Christian school and was close with my mom.

She's trying to keep you cut off from the rest of the world by keeping you there, she'd write. *Come on. I know you can't be that innocent.*

It went completely over my head that she was flirting with me.

I don't know what you mean.

Your whole angel act, she wrote. *I don't believe for a second that you've never cussed before.*

Well, one time at my grandfather's house I got my kite stuck in a tree, and I said, You damn kite!

She answered with an eye roll emoticon.

I didn't know it, but Mom was reading these texts whenever I'd leave my phone hanging around, and she began to develop an intense dislike for Darian. She was convinced that Darian was trying to corrupt me. But she couldn't say anything, because she didn't want me to know that she was checking my cell.

Mom wasn't the only one who disapproved of my new friend, either.

"Haven't you heard about her?" Andi asked me after she saw me chatting with her one day after dance class. "She's bad news."

"What do you mean?" I asked.

"Everyone knows she's made out with a ton of guys." She lowered her voice. "And I heard she cuts herself," she whispered.

In my thirteen-year-old mind, though, this only made her seem cooler. I didn't realize that she was totally tame compared to millions of other teenagers, but she was the first rebel I'd ever known, and while I'd never seen her kiss a boy, or seen any evidence of self-harm, she began to take on a larger-than-life quality for me. It was easier to believe Andi's rumors than just ask Darian what was true. And in a way, I didn't even want to know—I liked the mystery of Darian's life, and I liked that she was poking holes into the way I viewed what was acceptable behavior. She was just being who she was and not caring what people thought of her, something I was starting to desperately wish I could do myself. I chalked Andi's warnings up to jealousy over my having a new friend, but made sure to spend extra time with Andi so she didn't feel left out. But she never came near me when I was talking with Darian.

After a few months of being friends with Darian, both of our troupes were asked to perform on a Carnival Cruise. It was a pretty cool situation—it was a seven-day trip, and we had to do only one show on the boat, so all of our families basically got a fun vacation.

Before the cruise Mom took me shopping and bought all these girly clothes like tube tops and denim skirts. Along with my five new outfits, I snuck a couple of pairs of cargo shorts and some T-shirts into my bag, and those were all I wore the entire trip.

Our dance troupe would practice on board for a couple of hours each day—the show was scheduled for the fourth day of the cruise—and we just got to hang out the rest of the time. Wes became obsessed with Darian's boobs. He took a cell phone video of her dancing during one of our training sessions, and it's just a ten-minute shot of a headless Darian, with her breasts jiggling up and down.

After rehearsal Darian and I would sneak off. We'd do things like eat meals together and explore the ship. We would roughhouse in the hallway, and she'd mock punch me in the shoulder or pull my hair.

"Stop it," I'd say, taking a timid swipe back at her.

"That all you got?" she'd ask, and give me another friendly shove.

The more she pushed me, the more I started to laugh and tussle back. We'd put each other in headlocks and fall to the ground, rolling in the way of elderly couples who'd *tsssk* at us as they made their way to one of the ship's many dining rooms. I can remember the thrill of it—the body contact made me feel amazing and warm. I genuinely didn't recognize it as anything flirtatious or sexual. All I knew was that I wanted to touch her. I was so excited to have a new friend. Andi hadn't been able to make this trip because of a family wedding, and after being such a loner at school, all of the body contact made hanging out with my new companion that much more thrilling. I was starved for friendship, and every touch—every stray brush of her arm or hand on my back—sent a dizzying rush through me.

We started staying up late at night, finding hidden corners on the boat's outer decks that looked out at the ocean. The vast sky exploded with stars, and the moon's reflection created a clear path of light on the water. It looked like a road forward. I didn't know it at the time, but Darian was already out to her family and close friends as bisexual. But as she acknowledges now, she called herself bi then only because she wasn't quite ready to fully admit to being homosexual.

Conversations under the moonlight on the ocean tend to get deep fast—it's just the nature of the environment. There's something about being surrounded by water that makes you want to spill secrets. Maybe it's some sort of subconscious awareness that as beautiful as the ocean is, it's also deadly, so it forces confessions. But you can't confess things you don't already know, and as much as Darian suspected that I probably liked girls, and as much as she gently nudged the topic, I wouldn't give anything up, because I didn't even realize it myself.

"So, what do you think about gay people?" she asked one night.

"I think being gay is bad," I said, before I could even stop myself. For all of my burgeoning questions about Christianity at Lincoln, that was one idea that had been drilled so hard into my brain that the words just slipped out. But they felt immediately wrong, and I could tell she disapproved of my answer.

We were quiet for a minute.

"I don't think that it's wrong," she finally said. "So, what kind of guys do you like?"

"Oh—uh, you know, clean cut," I stammered. "Um, shaggy brown hair."

I didn't even realize that I was contradicting myself. I had no idea what to tell her, and couldn't understand why she wanted to talk about guys to begin with. "No tattoos," I added.

"No tattoos?" she said, and laughed. "That's exactly what I *do* like. Give me someone rough, with piercings."

Since she was so specific about what she liked, I felt like I needed to have a better answer for her. That night when I got to my stateroom, I did a Google image search on my phone for "cute guys" so I'd be better prepared to discuss them with her.

The next morning I showed her some pictures of generically handsome male models and pop stars, and for the rest of the trip, we developed this weird game where whenever one of us saw a guy that was remotely good-looking, we'd call, "Dibs!"

It makes me cringe to think about it now, but I understand why we did it. Even if it wasn't directed specifically at each other, we were exerting sexuality, despite it being a false representation of what we really wanted. By pretending to like these random guys, it kept the spark of attraction—however subconscious on my part—charged between us. It was like the G-rated version of two closeted teenage guys looking at a *Playboy* together, and brushing hands when they both reached to turn a page at the same time. It created electricity, a bond. She even casually brought up masturbation during our last late-night deck talk before the trip ended, and I thought, *Oh my God, I'm not the only one who does that?*

It was the most intimate conversation I'd ever had with someone, and even though I didn't realize it in the moment, it knocked down the last wall I'd built against her.

On the morning that we disembarked, I found her standing next to her bags and her family near the gangplank. I hugged her good-bye, and the moment my arms circled her body, I knew something was different.

I didn't want to let go.

I'd never experienced anything like it before and had no idea what to do, so I just held on. And she held me back, until I heard Mom calling me. I let go and stepped back, and it felt like I'd left something with her. I was flushed, and muttered

"Good-bye" before turning and practically running away.

We were on different flights home, and I obsessed about her the entire plane ride. I replayed every sentence of every conversation we'd had, felt the press of her chest against mine. My clothes even still smelled like the Victoria's Secret floral body lotion that she always wore.

I texted her the second we landed.

Remember when I hugged you before we left? There was something different about that.

Her response: *I know exactly what you mean.*

We continued to text over the next few days, and agreed that we needed to see each other again as soon as possible. About a week after the cruise, we got our chance—a huge heavy metal festival rolled into town. It was one of those mega tours, with eight different bands playing, like Disturbed, Avenged Sevenfold, and Halestorm. Darian was a lot more familiar with the music than I was, but the performances were hardly the point of going. I *needed* to see her.

Mom agreed to let me go, and even drove Darian and me to the Bank of Oklahoma Center, a huge stadium where all the major headline bands play. The line to get in seemed to stretch forever, and the crowd was packed with dudes with chains flapping from the belt loops on their black jeans. Spiky Mohawks sifted through the throngs like shark fins, and skinheads with tattooed faces openly smoked joints and scowled. The sounds of beer bottles smashing and people shouting or chanting lyrics surrounded us, but Darian and I were in our own private bubble, just talking and staring into each other's eyes. We stood in that line for almost three hours before the doors finally opened and the crowd spilled inside. Angry mosh pits formed out of nowhere, like fire ants swarming up from their underground nests, and we moved off to the side to avoid elbows to the face. But it wasn't scary—it was *alive*. We nodded our heads along with the music—timidly, compared to the furiously bobbing necks around us, but still inhaled every bit of energy in the arena. I felt like I had a contact high from the scent of weed in the air. Lights flashed, blinding us, and underneath the smoke it smelled like sweat and booze and heaven.

Our shoulders and elbows were pressed tight together, and every few minutes Darian and I would look at each other and hold the gaze. She was wearing a small, heart-shaped necklace that she'd chew on before letting it drop back down to her neck, and it would wet her lips slightly as it glided out of her mouth.

I'd never seen that look before, the one that meant, *I want to kiss you*. But I still recognized it in her eyes. I wanted to kiss her, too—it felt like the intimacy we'd shared on the boat, but amplified a million times, and the surreal environment only made it stronger. Both of us held back, though. We were still too scared, despite all the wild abandon surrounding us. But I think it was the peace we felt with each other in the midst of all that chaos that cemented us.

"I like you," I finally said. "I mean, I *like* like you."

"I do too," she said.

We pressed our shoulders even closer and slipped our hands together while they were sandwiched between our sides, so that no one could see. Not that anyone would have cared, but this was dangerous new territory for me, something to be kept hidden. I didn't yet feel the injustice of that necessity to hide—it was all still too new in my own brain. I needed to process my own reaction to these feelings before I could worry about how the rest of the world would respond.

By the time the concert ended, I was near deaf from the blasting speakers, and had to squint my eyes against the sudden brightness of the room after the lights went up. We reluctantly stepped away from each other, the spell momentarily broken as we made our way out to the parking lot and Mom's waiting car.

When we dropped her off, Darian nudged me with her knee. "Bye," she said. And then just sat there, not moving, staring at me.

"Yeah, okay, bye," I said. I wanted to kiss her *so bad*. She continued to stare for a few more moments before getting out and closing the door.

"That was weird," Mom muttered.

From that point forward it was on. We decided that the night of the concert was our anniversary. But since neither of us had a driver's license, and she lived on the other side of Tulsa, getting to actually see each other presented a problem. There was dance class twice a week, but it hardly gave us any sort of privacy. We went old-school and wrote each other letters talking about how much we liked each other, and we'd surreptitiously pass them off during class. Seeing her and not being able to stand too close to her or hold her hand was agony.

One night Andi caught me slipping a letter to Darian. "What's that all about?" she asked, sounding slightly hurt.

"Oh," I said, trying to think fast. "We spent a lot of time together on that cruise and she's, um, having some boyfriend troubles. I'm just trying to cheer her up."

"She seems like she can handle herself," Andi mumbled as we packed up our bags. I let the comment slide, too nervous to say anything else in case Andi heard something in my voice that would betray my real feelings about Darian. I wanted to talk to Andi about what was going on so badly, but she was *way* too religious. I knew she'd never accept the idea of Darian and me as a couple, and I didn't want to lose her as my best friend. It didn't occur to me at all that a real best friend would never do that.

Dividing lines were rapidly forming in the relationships with all the people in my life, though. I felt like I was a different person for everyone—the perfect child for Mom; the God-loving student at Lincoln; the dutiful dance student at Moore's; Andi's innocent best friend; and suddenly and most important, Darian's . . . girlfriend? But I hated that word because it had the word "girl" in it, and so I refused to use it. Luckily it was enough for her that we were secretly together. She was mature enough to not need that label to prove that we were in love.

At first all of these different roles were easy for me to juggle. I was caught up in the newness of it, and for a little while I got good at swapping them out like Halloween masks. The feeling wouldn't last long, though.

A few weeks after the cruise, we had an evening

performance in front of an audience in Claremore, a small town about thirty minutes away from my house but kind of close to Aunt Susan's place and Papa and Gigi's farm. It gave me the perfect opportunity to invite Darian to spend the night at Susan's with the rest of my cousins. I didn't mention the sleepover to Andi.

After the show, Darian and I headed to Susan's and tore through the house with my cousins, gorged on snacks, had pillow fights, and played hide-and-seek in the backyard. Late at night Cheyenne, Darian, and I all piled onto Amanda's bed with her to watch *Pirates of the Caribbean*. Cheyenne eventually stumbled off to her room, rubbing her eyes. On the other side of the bed, Amanda started breathing deeply as she fell asleep.

Darian and I stared at each other. It was the closest we'd been to being alone together since our nights on the cruise ship's deck. I wanted so bad to lean in and kiss her, but I was still too scared. Instead I gently placed the back of my hand against her mouth. I had no idea what I was doing. It was instinct, almost as if there were this one last barrier that I needed to put up between us. I needed some sort of symbolic permission from her that it was safe to finally break open this part of me.

She began to kiss my hand, and I melted.

We made out, gently and quietly. We moved to the floor so we wouldn't disturb Amanda, and kept our hands on top of our clothes. I didn't want her going anywhere near my breasts, and I maneuvered her away every time she tried to touch them. It kept taking me out of the moment and made it hard to concentrate on the fact that I was making out with someone for the first time in my life. But I finally relaxed into it when she got the message that I was much more interested in exploring her body than having her discover mine.

I spent the next few days in a haze, grinning all the time. Mom even commented on how happy I seemed, and while part of me really wanted to tell her the reason why, I couldn't do it. How could she understand what was going on, when I hardly understood it myself? I couldn't tell her that I was gay, because I didn't feel gay. But making out with a girl and loving it *made* me gay. I kept going around in circles in my brain and couldn't land on an answer, an identity.

All I did know was that I couldn't wait to see Darian again at our next dance class. I started arriving fifteen minutes early to class, as she was finishing up with the younger kids, so we could steal a little bit of time together before my class started. One night, when no one was looking, she grabbed my hand and led me to the back, into a small cinder block room that housed the building's only water fountain. She pushed me up against the wall and kissed me. I was shocked by how brazen she was—anybody could have walked in at any second—but it didn't matter. I'd never given up control like that to another person in my life, and it felt so weirdly freeing.

We heard someone coming down the hallway, and quickly pulled apart, taking turns at the fountain as if nothing had happened. I was lighter on my feet that night than ever before.

We knew that the water fountain room was far too risky for clandestine make-out sessions, so we'd sneak around to the back of the building. It faced an empty parking lot and a green garbage Dumpster, and there was a small indentation in the wall where all the electrical, gas, and water piping that led inside was housed. We'd press up against that small corner, out of sight from anyone, and go at it.

We managed to get away with it for about two weeks. I got Mom to drive me to class earlier and earlier every Tuesday and Thursday, telling her that I wanted to hang out with a friend. When we'd come back inside after fooling around, we'd still be grinning and flirting with each other. There was obvious sexual tension between us, and everyone must have felt or seen it. And since Darian was already sort of out as bi, she had a few friends in Shockwave who knew exactly what was going on—despite the fact that Darian had promised me she wouldn't tell anyone about us. The fact that she eventually did ended up being a blessing, though.

One night when we were outside as usual, we heard a voice whisper, "Someone's coming!" I didn't realize it at the time, but it was one of Darian's friends trying to warn us. We pulled away fast, and Darian went pale. We were furiously trying to wipe off our faces when my dance instructor came flying around the corner of the building. She looked *pissed*.

"You guys can't hang out back here," she snapped. She was looking us up and down with disgust, and even though we hadn't *technically* been caught together, I knew that she knew. And I knew that I was screwed.

7

I stumbled my way through dance class, totally unable to keep up. Andi kept shooting me concerned glances. I knew she could tell something was going on, and I avoided her eyes, pretending instead to concentrate on my feet, but I might as well have been clogging on a floor covered with marbles, for all the skill I was demonstrating.

I tried to avoid eye contact with Darian when she and the rest of her troupe filed in for the last half hour of my class. A couple of her friends were staring at me with worried looks. They must have heard what had happened, and I panicked that the news would start circulating, even though I knew that Darian wouldn't be friends with anyone she couldn't trust. I didn't say good-bye to either her or Andi once we were done, and hightailed it out the door. Mom was waiting in the car right outside, and she didn't say a word the entire ride home. I kept my mouth shut too. She was acting so weird that I knew she had to know what had happened. *Did the studio call her?* I wondered. I wasn't about to ask.

She barely spoke during dinner. Wes was acting like his normal, loud, oblivious self, singing random songs he made up about the broccoli we were eating, which helped ease the tension a little. I went up to my room after we ate and sat on my bed, debating how I should handle the situation.

I went downstairs to her room and sat on her bed while she rustled around in her bathroom, getting ready to go to sleep.

"Just wanted to say good night," I called out to her. Her phone was on her nightstand, and it was still lit up from a recent text. I rolled over and picked it up to read it, and saw that it was from Kelli, Andi's mom.

It said: *She's not gonna go and say outright that your child is gay.*

Mom came out of the bathroom and saw the phone in my hand. I started to ask her what the text meant, and that was when she exploded.

"Everyone is going around saying that you and Darian were kissing out behind the dance studio!" she shrieked. "The studio owner called *Kelli* at her house to gossip about it, because she didn't want to tell me herself. What is going on?"

I hadn't expected this to go well, but the wrath in her voice terrified me. I had hoped that maybe it was something we could talk honestly about, but I realized in that instant that anything I said was going to fall on totally deaf ears. She was livid.

So I denied it.

"What?" I asked, all innocent-like. "We were just hanging out!"

"No one would just make something like that up," she

yelled. "And everyone knows Darian is a lesbian. She's, what, two years older than you? Did she force you to do this?"

"Nothing happened! She's just a friend and we were talking!"

"About what?" she demanded.

Damn. I hadn't thought that far ahead. "Dance stuff," I blurted out. "She was, uh, helping me out with my moves."

That came out wrong.

Mom narrowed her eyes. "Why can't you do that in the studio?"

"I don't know! Mom, it's no big deal!"

"Oh, it's a big deal. They all think you're a lesbian now. I know you're not, but they might believe you are."

That stopped me cold. I knew for sure by that point that I had to be gay or bi, because I loved kissing Darian, but a lesbian? That meant a gay *woman*, and that felt utterly wrong. I was more like . . . a gay tomboy or something. Like a tomgay.

I started to feel really dizzy and weird. I couldn't wrap my brain around what I was feeling.

"I'm not a lesbian, Mom," I said. "And I can't believe you'd listen to a bunch of dumbass dance instructors over me."

"You're grounded," she shouted as I stormed out. "And I'm coming to every single one of your classes from now on to make sure you go to class and stay inside!"

She kept her promise, and created an entire narrative in her mind to explain what must have happened—that Darian was a seductress, a horny older woman desperate to get into my chaste, virginal pants. The whole thing was even more infuriating because I knew that Darian had told her mom about us from the very beginning, and Darian's mom was completely cool with it.

Mom needed to sit in on the classes for only about a week before the instructors set down an edict that no student was allowed to come to classes early or to stay late. It felt like everyone's eyes were constantly on us, and not being able to speak to her was torture. But it was comforting to know that she must have been feeling the exact same way I was.

Being at home or in the car with Mom was agonizing. She'd give me death stares, trying to make me confess. But I kept up my innocent act. Andi had asked me right away if what her mom had heard was true, and even though she was my best friend, I couldn't confess the truth. But I could tell that she didn't believe my protests, and she began to act wary and distant whenever I saw her at the studio. Worse, she started sending me texts of Bible verses:

Thou shalt not lie with mankind, as with womankind: it is abomination.

For this cause God gave them up unto vile affections: for even their women did change the natural use into that which is against nature.

Know ye not that the unrighteous shall not inherit the kingdom of God? Be not deceived: neither fornicators, nor idolaters, nor adulterers, nor effeminate, nor abusers of themselves with mankind.

I could hardly be accused of being effeminate.

None of these passages were new to me—Lincoln had made sure of that. I didn't need reminders sent to my phone telling me that the Bible thought I was evil; it had been drummed into my head already at school. And sometimes I wondered if maybe I *should* break things off with Darian. Maybe I *was* going to go to hell. But at the same time I couldn't understand how something as incredible as loving someone could be a bad thing. It didn't make sense. But then guilt would creep back in and I'd consider dumping her. And an hour later I'd be missing Darian so much, it would make me physically ache. I was a wreck.

About ten days after Darian and I got busted, Wes and I went to Susan's after school to visit our cousins. Susan was still at work, so I sat down at her desk and started scribbling a letter to Darian.

I miss you so much, I wrote. *It's killing me that we can't be together. I just want to be able to kiss you, and I don't know what to do.*

I was sticking it inside an envelope when Cheyenne suddenly burst into the room, followed by Dewayne, chasing her. I shoved the letter under a stack of other papers to hide it, planning to pick it up later, and took off after them into the backyard to join the race and play around.

Mom and Susan came home from work as the sun was setting. I stayed in the backyard with the rest of the kids until I heard Mom's car horn honking from the driveway. I called shotgun and climbed into the passenger seat while Wes muttered and grumbled about being stuck in the back. As Mom reversed slowly out into the road, I glanced down and saw a pile of papers shoved down between the seats.

The corner of my letter to Darian was sticking out.

While she was still stretching her head over her shoulder checking for cars, I snatched the letter and shoved it into my pocket. I panicked the entire ride home. Susan must have seen it, read it, and then given it to Mom. I cursed myself for being stupid enough to forget it, and cursed Susan for narcing on me.

When we got home, I ran inside. Mom followed with the stack of papers and was rifling through them anxiously.

"Did you see an envelope anywhere?" she asked. "I'm missing one."

"Nope," I said as innocently as I could. I could feel the tension in the room building as she glared at me.

"Are you sure? It was right here with the rest, next to you," she said.

And just like that, I realized I couldn't keep it up anymore. I was exhausted, tired of lying, and furious that we were having this standoff when we each knew exactly what was going on but neither would say it. I was done playing games.

"Fine," I yelled. "I kissed her!"

"I *know* you did," she yelled back. "It's on *paper*. I saw the letter! I don't know why you think you could keep lying to me! Is that really what you want people to think of you?"

"What is that supposed to mean?"

She sighed. "I just don't understand why you had to go and do that *there*. The place we've been going all of our lives."

"Where else was I supposed to?" I asked. "She doesn't drive, and you've made it clear that you don't like her."

"She's too old for you," she said. "And she's taking advantage of you. Listen, I get it. I think girls are pretty too. But I don't *kiss* them."

"Well, I do." I mumbled.

"You're *not* gay," she said.

"I never said I was," I yelled. "I don't know. I guess I'm bi. I like Darian. That's it."

"No," she said, in this calm and infuriating way, like she was the only one who could know the truth about these things. "You've just never been in a relationship before, and Darian is showering you with all of this attention. *She's* making you feel this way."

I ran out of the kitchen before I could say something that would really get me in trouble. When I was halfway up the stairs, she shouted, "You are not allowed to see her outside of class, *ever!*"

Andi finally texted me an actual question, instead of hiding what she wanted to know behind the Bible.

Just tell me exactly. What is going on?

I think I'm bi, I wrote.

This is too much, she wrote back. *I can't deal with you anymore.*

I had known it was coming, but that didn't make the end of our friendship sting any less. It killed me that Andi couldn't use her incredible imagination to see a world beyond the hateful religious one she lived in.

Except for my cousins, I now officially had no friends.

Darian and I still managed to pass letters off to each other at the studio, and that's how I found out that Mom had gotten Darian's mother's number and invited her to lunch.

She took my mom out for soup, Darian wrote. *And basically told her that she needed to keep me away from you.*

I was mortified, but I couldn't confront Mom about it. If I did that, then she would know that I was still secretly keeping in touch with Darian. I became more determined than ever to figure out a way to see her.

One day Wes and I were helping Dad run some errands near his house in Catoosa, and he asked me about Darian.

"Your mom says you have this new friend that she isn't so into," he said.

"What else did she say?" I asked, bracing myself.

"Nothing really, just mentioned that she didn't like her much."

I realized that he had no idea what was actually going on. Like always, Mom was keeping the ins and outs of raising us on her own shoulders. And now that Dad was away from the house, she had even *less* of a reason to keep him informed about the drama of our daily lives. He had settled comfortably into his role of the casual father—happy to hang around for holidays, mall trips, and outdoor fun, but that was about it. She had no reason—or incentive—to start involving him *more* in our lives now.

"Darian's not bad at all," I said. "In fact, she's really cool. I think you'd like her. I don't know why Mom is being so weird about it."

"She's got really big boobs," Wes piped up from the back-seat.

"Think I can stay at your house this weekend?" I asked. "I feel like I need a break from home."

"I wanna come too!" Wes said.

Dad was surprised. We never asked to stay over—the woods and backyard around Mom's house were just way more fun to be at on the weekends. He immediately said yes, as long as Mom was okay with it. And she was—I think she needed a break from me, too.

As soon as we got there that Friday, I asked him if Darian could come and spend the night. "Sure," he said, shrugging.

I called Darian and told her what was going on. "I don't know," she said. "My mom was pretty freaked out by all the stuff your mom said about keeping me away from you. I don't think she'll let me."

"Tell her to call my dad," I said. "He'll give her permission."

Darian had a dance show that night, and we picked her up right after. From the second she arrived, we couldn't keep our hands off each other whenever we had a second alone, but we had to be diligent and make sure that we could always hear Dad and Wes in some other part of the house. It was after midnight before they finally said good night, and we stayed up watching a movie for a while, waiting for the house to settle and grow quiet before we headed off to the bedroom.

I wanted to do everything with her, but I was so self-conscious about my body that I refused to take my underwear and sports bra off. She kept trying to peel them away, but I resisted until she gave up and let me explore her. As new and wild as it all was, I couldn't shake the weirdness I felt about my own body. There were movements I felt I was supposed to be making, but there was no equipment to do it with.

I'd recently started having dreams that I was screwing girls with my very own dick. The dreams weren't happening every night, but at least twice a week. The dreams were sort of like the ones you have when you remember that you can fly, and it's always this wonderful surprise. *Oh, right,* you think. *How could I have forgotten that I have this ability?*

But now that I was with someone in reality, I felt more strongly than ever the absence of something between my legs. Thanks to the dreams, I knew what I was missing out on, how this was *supposed* to all feel.

But with the armor of my underwear still cloaking me, I could at least pretend. I got her naked and did everything to her that I'd been dreaming about doing to a girl for so long.

Well, almost everything.

We spent the next day catching up, watching movies, raiding the fridge, and fending off Wesley. At one point he finally left the house to help my dad outside with some yard work, and we immediately grabbed each other and started making out on the couch.

"What are you *doing*?"

We leapt apart, and saw Wes standing in the doorway, looking confused.

"We were just wrestling," I said as Darian covered her face.

"No you weren't," he said.

"Yes, we were," I said. "Get out of here. Go back outside."

"Didn't look like wrestling to me," he grumbled as he wandered off.

After that we didn't dare try anything else. Dad drove her home later that day, and I spent the rest of the weekend in a daze. Finally doing so many of the things to a girl that I had dreamed about had given me some semblance of power over my body. Even if I felt like my body wasn't the one I was supposed to have, I was at least learning that there were things I could do with it.

I knew it was pointless to try to hide from Mom that Darian had stayed the night. When she picked me up Monday morning, she asked how my weekend had been.

"Darian slept over," I said casually, as if it were no big deal.

I watched with a mix of awe and dread as her face got redder and her eyes grew wider. I was scared of her reaction, but at the same time I just didn't really care anymore. She could do whatever she wanted to punish me. It wasn't going to stop me from loving Darian.

She exploded. "YOU ARE GROUNDED! How DARE you go behind my back like this! I told you, you are not allowed to see that girl EVER!"

I stared at the passing houses and tuned her rant out. A small smile danced on my face as I recalled every single detail of our night together.

When Dad found out that I'd been busted kissing Darian at the dance studio and I'd manipulated his trust, he was pissed, but since Mom yelled at him about it as much as she had yelled at me, he went easy. He told Mom that I was probably just going through a lesbian phase and that I didn't even know what I was doing. I considered trying to talk with him seriously about what was going on, but then he told me that I was "too pretty to be a lesbian." I pretty much shut him out after that. He clearly wasn't ready to understand anything I was going through.

Mom took away my phone when she grounded me, so I was completely cut off from the world except for school and dance. I started to get seriously depressed, pining for Darian. I had no appetite and began to lose a ton of weight. We were back to slipping notes to each other if we had a chance between dance classes, and enlisting the help of her friends as go-betweens if everyone's eyes were on us. We spoke in code—we'd write the phrase "three words" instead of "I love you," in case anyone ever got their hands on one of our letters. And whenever we saw each other, we'd subtly hold up three fingers to each other to mean the same, so that we could talk without speaking.

Out of nowhere, Susan came to my rescue after picking me up from school when Mom had a meeting that she couldn't get out of.

"Listen," she told me. "I know that things are bad between you and your mom right now, and I just want you to know that I am on your side. She will come around eventually, I promise. And in the meantime, if you ever need to get away, my house is always open to you. And to Darian, too."

I was grateful but shocked. She and Mom were really close,

and for Susan to go behind Mom's back like that was huge. Especially after I saw Mom's reaction toward Dad after he had let me spend the night with Darian. But more important, her support reinforced in my mind that I was the one in the right. There was nothing wrong with my feelings for Darian.

I thanked her and immediately took her up on the offer. Whenever Darian and I came over, Susan would cook all my favorite foods, such as steak, or spaghetti with chicken, to try to help me get my weight back up.

We'd always wait until the house was asleep before fooling around. While Susan was cool with us being together, she expected that under her roof everything would stay respectfully PG.

But come on! I mean, we were horny teenagers in love who were being forcibly kept apart! We were going to take advantage of every second of alone time we could get.

This went on for a couple of months before Cheyenne eventually walked in on us one night and told on me. Susan was pissed that I'd taken advantage of her hospitality, and the invitations stopped after that.

Darian and I were back to square one. I'd gotten my phone back, but Darian knew that Mom checked it, so she bought me a prepaid cell so I could make calls in secret. But I was too scared that Mom would find it, so Darian used it instead, to communicate with me. That way I could get texts from a number that Mom wouldn't recognize.

Still, texts weren't enough. Those little electronic shots in the dark, messages telling me that I was loved and needed, would help me temporarily, but after the initial thrill of getting one, the coldness in my life would start to creep back in. I had to delete the ones that were too obvious, in case Mom checked my phone, so I didn't even have words to look back at for comfort. Being with Darian had woken up a part of me that had always been there under the surface, slumbering. Getting such a small taste of what I wanted from my life, and then having it ripped away from me almost immediately, was such a cruel punishment for doing nothing except being born the way I was. It all started to take a horrible psychic toll on me. My depression grew worse every day, and I withdrew so much—to the point where I wasn't even talking whenever I was at home—that Mom took me to the doctor.

"Are you depressed?" he asked.

"Yes."

"About what?"

As if I'd tell you. "I don't know. It's just a feeling. Or a non-feeling. I don't care about anything."

He put me on Prozac, which helped for about a week in that it gave me a buzzy sort of energy. But it faded quickly, and soon Mom started having to drag me from bed in the morning. I had no interest in facing a world that didn't want to face me—because it wasn't just my own mother who was telling me that my feelings were wrong. I got it every day in school, too. The brief confidence boost I'd gotten from Susan's support was long gone, and the Bible classes at Lincoln seemed to be making more and more references about what a huge sin being gay was. I wondered if some edict had come down from the administration that the teachers needed to be more active in spewing that hate. Or maybe it had always been there that much, and I was just beginning to tune in to it more.

One day a teacher went on a tirade about gay marriage, repeating all the same old Bible quotes I'd heard a million times before, the same ones Andi had texted me. I raised my hand.

"But aren't we supposed to be preaching love?"

"We do preach love," he said. "The love of Jesus."

"I know, but didn't Jesus make a big deal about not discriminating against people? He loved everyone equally."

"Ah HA!" the teacher exclaimed, as if I'd just answered some big mystery. "Yes! But Jesus loved the *sinner*, not the sin."

Not that tired old crap again, I thought. I was actually disappointed in him. I wished that just once my teachers would engage in a topic without simply using as the basis of their argument something someone else had once written down ages ago.

In the past I'd always focused my frustration on the *students* at Lincoln as the problem; I thought they were the ones who didn't represent what true Christianity was. But it was the institution itself that was a perverted version of the essential point of the Bible—love thy neighbor. *Of course* the students here were jerks—they were being taught to discriminate.

I know it sounds like such an obvious realization to have, but I had only just turned fourteen.

When I left school that day, I took a good look at all the

buildings around me, and the mega church that stood up on the slight hill above us. There was so much money being pumped into this place—money that could actually help those who needed it. Instead they used it to employ people who created more people who believed that being gay was going to send me straight to the devil.

But the thing is, I knew that what I was feeling was beyond being gay. The label still didn't feel right, which made the whole mess even more confusing and scary. I was still regularly having dreams that I had a penis. There were times in them when I'd look down and see it there between my legs and feel such an incredible wave of relief. *Oh, that's right,* I'd think. *It was there all along.* And then I'd wake up. I had no idea what was wrong with me, and I felt like I had no place in the world.

I decided to do some research, hoping to find someone— anyone—who had the same sorts of dreams and feelings as me. The only time I had unsupervised access to the Internet was when I was at Papa and Gigi's house. I stopped playing outside with my cousins and started holing up in my grand-parents' back office, searching YouTube for videos from gay people. I knew that "LGBT" was the phrase to search for to find the smart, personal stories, as opposed to just typing in "gay" and getting hundreds of videos of pretty boys lip-synching to pop songs in their bedrooms.

And I knew that the *T* stood for "trans," but I didn't have any clue what the word even meant.

One day a recommended video popped up along the side, a video journal by someone named Skylarkeleven.

Something about the guy's face felt familiar, like I'd seen him somewhere before, so I clicked on it.

That was when everything changed.

The video was called "One year on testosterone comparison." It had been made by a guy with short, tousled blond hair and a Peter Pan kind of vibe—very animated and self-confident, but not in a jerk sort of way. He was bouncy and excited, and I soon saw why. He began showing clips of videos he'd posted in the past, just before and after starting something called hormone therapy. He was getting regular injections of testosterone, prescribed by a doctor in order to help his body become more masculine. The video tracked his evolution over a year into a progressively deeper-voiced boy.

He was what I wanted to be.

He was who I *was*.

He even had the same haircut I fantasized about.

I blew Google up that night, researching everything I could about being transgender, and with everything I read, I clicked a mental check mark next to every question I'd ever had about myself.

Did I feel that I was something other than just gay? Yes.

Did I have a feeling that I'd been born into the wrong body? Yup.

Did I relate strongly to a gender identity that wasn't the one I was born with? *Hell* yeah.

I saw countless photos of trans men who had gotten their breasts removed by having what they called "top surgery." I thought my eyes were going to pop out of my head. It had never even occurred to me that I could just get *rid* of them. It seemed so obvious, and I was almost mad at myself for never before realizing that was an option. But really, how could I have known?

I seethed with jealousy at every photo of flat pecs. Even the ones who had large surgery scars looked better than anything I had ever thought possible for myself. I learned the word "cisgender," or "cis," as the proper way to define a person whose gender identity matches the gender of the body they were born with. I loved knowing there was actually a specific vocabulary word that described people who *weren't* like me, as opposed to *me* being the "other."

It's hard to describe what it all actually felt like. I imagine it's sort of similar to having some horrible disease for years, and then one day your doctor calls you and says, "We found the cure!" Or if an amnesiac suddenly recovers all his memories. Or like playing a video game where you spend forever trying to solve the right puzzle, and then when you do, a hidden gate you hadn't noticed before suddenly swings open. *That* feeling—only times a trillion.

When I finally emerged from Papa and Gigi's back office, I felt like I was floating. I was bursting with new information, *priceless* information that finally explained everything that was wrong with me. I wanted to know more and more and more—everything I possibly could about being transgender. But at least I was already brimming with enough knowledge to understand that there was suddenly a path laid out before me, where there had been none before. I now had a clear set of steps that could help guide me to becoming the person I knew I was.

The question now, though: Who would go down that road with me?

I got to the end of the hallway and saw my family sitting in the living room, and suddenly my depression came crashing back onto my shoulders. The task at hand seemed impossible—how could I ever tell them that I wasn't actually a girl? Would they ever accept that? Papa and Gigi are really religious, and if religion says being gay is a sin, then I figured transgender people must have their very own suite in the ninth circle of hell. And Darian had recently come to the realization that she was an adamant lesbian, instead of just bisexual. She'd told me that she never wanted to be with a man. So what did that mean for us?

I'd finally discovered the truth about myself, but instead of it setting me free, I realized that things were actually probably about to get a whole lot worse.

8

Despite Darian's recent coming out as a full-on lesbian, I still knew that she was the only person I could tell right away about my discovery. But we were practically cut off from each other. Mom had pretty much confiscated my cell phone permanently after discovering a text from Darian that I'd forgotten to delete, so we'd have furtive phone conversations on my house's landline whenever possible. But I always had one ear out for Mom. Darian knew to stop talking and immediately hang up if it ever sounded like someone picked up the other line. Though I was never able to have a fully fleshed-out conversation with her about what I was going through, I was able to communicate the basics, and she was supportive and encouraging from the get-go. The idea that I was trans didn't faze her at all.

"I have a cousin who is engaged to a trans man," she said. "It doesn't change the way I feel about you."

The problem was, it started to change the way I felt about her. Darian was a lesbian, which meant she liked girls. Now that I knew I wasn't a girl, I wondered if my dating her would just continue to remind me that I was stuck in the body of one.

I watched all of Skylarkeleven's YouTube videos. I wondered if he realized just how lucky he was to have what seemed like such a strong support group around him. And some days, watching his freedom only intensified my feeling of isolation. I sent him a message, thanking him for putting up such incredibly personal videos, and letting him know how much they helped me. I checked every day for a response back, nervously opening my e-mail, only to feel my heart crash when there was nothing there. I understood, though. I knew I wasn't the only person he was helping, and he must have been slammed with tons of messages just like mine. Still, I desperately wanted an ally.

Sometimes entire weeks would go by when Darian and I wouldn't get to speak. And when we did, I'd vomit up so much repressed emotion that I started to scare her.

"I'm completely trapped," I said at one point. I had dragged our landline into a closet, since my mom was home, but talking to Darian was worth the risk. I knew I was starting to spiral. "And now that I know the truth, it almost makes it harder. I will never be able to be like Skylarkeleven. And school . . ."

"You'll be out of that hellhole in a few years," she said. "It will fly by, I promise. Like they say, it gets better. You'll be able to get out from under all this control and live the life you want."

Funny how people can say all the right things and it still

means nothing. I couldn't fathom a world outside the one I lived in. The depression turned to a dull numbness. Every single day became the same. I kept my headphones on constantly and listened to the song "Shake Me Down" by Cage the Elephant on repeat. *Eyes cast down,* I'd chant along in my mind. I became obsessed with how flat and hopeless the geographical landscape around us was. On the drive to school we'd pass by fields that stretched out forever into nothingness, and I'd picture myself walking out into one of them and never stopping.

One afternoon as we drove by the American Legion building, I noticed a group of uniformed teenagers marching in perfect unison, with rifles held over their shoulders. Suddenly they stopped, and the guns started spinning around their sides and backs like batons, with precision movements. The guns settled back onto their shoulders, and they continued their march forward.

"What is that all about?" I asked Mom, pointing.

"I think that's the Civil Air Patrol," she said, squinting at them. She started to swerve into the other lane, and quickly straightened the wheel. "I'm pretty sure they have a youth program. Is that something you'd be interested in?"

"Air patrol?" I asked. "Does that mean they let you fly planes?"

"We'll look it up when we get home," she said.

We learned that Civil Air Patrol, or CAP, is an offshoot of the United States Air Force and is open to pretty much anyone. It teaches about the history of flying, provides aerospace education, and trains people for dealing with emergency situations like plane crashes.

"I want in," I told Mom. There was something about how in control of themselves they'd looked that appealed to me on a very base level. And the idea of rescue missions and learning how to save people cut a small swath of light through the fog in my brain.

I filled out some background check forms and was accepted after about three weeks. My first squadron meeting was held at the air force base at Tulsa International Airport. When Mom dropped me off, I watched a small fighter plane speed down the runway and take off into the sky. I pictured myself in the cockpit, with the freedom to go anywhere. When you're up in the sky, who you are on the ground doesn't matter.

There were about twenty cadets in total, mostly guys, and I felt out of place at first, since I was the only person in civilian clothing. Everyone else was wearing uniforms and nametags.

"Fall in!" the squadron commander barked, and I took the end spot in the line that suddenly formed. I watched the way everyone was marching, and imitated them as we walked about half a mile to the airplane maintenance hangars and practiced more marching drills.

I loved it. I could make my body do exactly what I told it to. CAP allowed me to have an authority over my physicality that was otherwise completely absent from my life.

No one at CAP thought it was weird that I acted masculine. They even embraced the fact that I could keep up with the guys during physical exercise. I was issued a navy-blue air force suit with huge brass buttons, a nametag, a cadet badge, and a pointed flight cap. Men and women wore almost identical suits, so it was easy for me to pretend that I was just one of the guys. I learned to spin rifles like a pro. (They were plugged, so you couldn't actually shoot them.)

It was the perfect distraction, something to take my mind off the depression, off Darian, and off the truth of who I was.

But better than all of that, I started making friends.

I became really close with two guys in particular, Samuel, who was around my age, and Jon, who was several years older than me and already in college.

One weekend I invited them over, and we hiked down to the giant boulders behind my house. The cave I'd built between the rocks had started to come apart, and I had recently found a couple of copperheads living in the back of it, so I'd dismantled the whole thing and built a fire in the hole for good measure. I may be a huge animal lover, but I hate snakes.

"Let's build something here," I said.

"Like what?" Samuel asked.

I thought for a minute. I missed having a hideout, a little place to escape to, one that was all my own.

"A cabin," I decided.

We scrounged all the spare lumber we could find from the garage and built a basic frame out of two-by-fours. We hammered compressed wood panels onto the top and sides to make a roof and walls. A small hole cut into the front served as the entrance, so that it still felt sort of like a cave. I hung a towel over it that could be pushed aside to let in fresh air.

That night Samuel stayed over with me in the cabin. I'd been asked to join the CAP honor guard, the riflemen who honor fallen soldiers at official military ceremonies. The training was supposed to be really intense, and since Samuel was going to be one of my instructors, he kept me up all night with horror stories about the endurance tests, things like having to stay in a push-up position for ten straight minutes.

We woke up at dawn and cooked breakfast over a fire I built on the rocks, and from that day on, I was always inviting CAP friends over for campouts and bonfires down at the little cabin. It was the first time in my life that I had ever felt truly accepted by a group. The camaraderie helped cut through the loneliness of missing Darian. And while I was pretty sure that some of the guys from CAP might have had crushes on me, everyone was too professional to ever act on it. We were a team.

Hands down, the best part of CAP was getting to ride in the airplanes. I wasn't allowed to sit up front in the cockpit with the pilot, but I got to go on a bunch of orientation rides and sit in the back to watch practice missions for search and rescue operations. I paid close attention to all the instructions but would still find my mind drifting just a little, overpowered by the sheer wonder of flying. The small single-propeller Cessnas we flew were nothing like the impersonal giants that commercial airlines use. In one of those you may as well be on a bus— you hardly feel any relationship to the empty space outside.

But on the smaller planes, I felt like I was telling gravity to screw off. I was breaking the rules of nature, and getting away with it.

Jon and I grew especially close. I looked up to him like a big brother, and even found myself modeling certain masculine mannerisms after him. Little things, like the crisp way he tucked in his shirts. Catchphrases that he was always uttering started coming out of my mouth as well, and I watched how he moved his arms when he walked, as an example of how to swing my own. He started coming over every Wednesday night to sit around the fire and talk.

"I promise I'll take you flying with me someday," he said. "And when you're old enough, I'll help you get your pilot's license."

But despite how close we were, I never told him about Darian, or that I knew I was transgender. I was still too scared of those sides of myself to test them out on anyone.

Having friends again gave me confidence, though, and coupled with the joy I got from flying, I was able to partially pull myself out of my depression. I started excelling at school, making top grades. I wanted to prove to my teachers that I was a worthwhile human, even if they'd hate me if they knew what I was inside. So I worked hard, and kept my mouth shut whenever someone would call me a lesbian in the hallway, or make fun of the way I walked or spoke.

In fact, I got so good at faking the part of being a good Christian girl during my freshman year that I was awarded the Lincoln Spotlight Student of the Year Award, a plaque they gave out annually to one student in the high school for their exemplary work in fulfilling the school's three core priorities: Godly character, academic excellence, and extra-curricular activities. In that exact order.

Since things seemed to be going so well, Mom finally agreed to let me cut my hair. Not as short as I wanted—only to my shoulders—but it still meant nine inches off, and I knew it would make it even easier for me to hide the rest of it up in a hat.

She drove me to the same place where we'd always gotten our hair done, a place called Spalon, located in a strip mall and sandwiched between a Body by God health club on one side and an abandoned Jazzercise studio on the other. The stylist, Rachel, had known me for several years by then, and she knew how badly I'd always wanted to chop my hair off, so she understood what a big deal it was.

"If you're going this short, we should donate to Locks of Love," she said, and gathered my hair into a long ponytail. "You've got enough here for sure."

She picked up the shears.

"Ready?"

"Born ready," I said.

Mom suddenly bolted. "I'll wait outside," she choked.

Rachel patted me on the shoulder. "Don't worry, honey. She'll come around when she sees how good I'm going to make you look."

"Oh, I'm not worried," I said. "Do it already!"

The high-pitched shearing sound was just like I'd always imagined, and as soon as the chunk of hair was separated from my body, I felt my head drift upward, as if there were helium balloons tied to my ears. While my hair had been pulled back, I had seen my true, short-haired self in the mirror, and I felt a slight twinge of disappointment when the remaining strands fell back down around and settled on the tops of my shoulders. But the lightness felt incredible, and I shook my head back and forth a few times to get used to it. I couldn't stop grinning.

My happiness was short-lived, though. I got a text from Darian's secret phone, asking me to call her as soon as I could. I snuck away the first chance I got.

"I'm quitting dance," Darian told me as soon as she picked up.

I let that sink in for a minute. "But that's the only time I ever get to see you," I said.

"I know," she said. "But I can't take those homophobic rednecks anymore. They don't say anything out loud, but I know they've hated me ever since you and I got busted together. They treat me like dirt, even though I'm good at what I do there. It's all because I love you. And we are *paying* these people money to go there! I just can't be a part of it anymore."

"And what about me?" I asked, my voice sounding far away.

"You're going to escape someday," she said. "And I'll be waiting. But our next recital is going to be my last one."

After we hung up, I thought hard about everything she'd said about the dance studio. As much as it killed me that I wouldn't get to see her, I couldn't argue with any of her points. In fact, the more I thought about it, the angrier I got. For my family it wasn't just the dance studio we were giving money to—it was my school. Their hard-earned cash was going straight into the pockets of people who wanted me to burn.

I knew the time had come to tell Mom that I was transgender. CAP had been serving as a good distraction from having to face reality, but it was also helping me build up the confidence to own up to who I really was.

I figured since the school year was ending, we'd have the whole rest of the summer for her to process it, and hopefully let me begin transitioning. I considered suggesting we go out to lunch somewhere and I'd tell her there, so she couldn't freak out because we'd be in public. Or maybe I'd build a fire in the backyard and tell her over the crackling flames, surrounded by nature. Perhaps whatever magic energy the woods held for me would rub off on her, too, and make it all okay.

In the end I chose a highway off-ramp.

We were driving to the studio for our end-of-year recital, the last time I'd see Darian for any sort of foreseeable future. As we curved down the road toward the thruway, I felt my stomach drop, as if we were free-falling on a roller coaster.

"Mom, do you know what 'transgender' is?"

She was silent as she merged into the traffic.

It's happening, I thought, and started to tremble. *It's actually happening.*

I held my breath, waiting for her to reply.

"I think so," she said, her eyes straight ahead. "But why don't you explain it to me."

"It's when a boy feels like a girl, and he changes his body

to match his mind. Or when a girl feels like a guy, and she does what she can to be male," I said, before I could lose my nerve. "That's what I am."

I was too scared to look at her. I watched the white divider lines on the road disappear underneath the front wheels, charting our progression.

"So you want to be a boy," she said finally. Her voice was flat.

"Yeah."

"So you want a penis."

"Well, yeah. That's part of it. But it's a lot more than just that."

Neither of us said another word for the rest of the ride. When we got to the studio, I left the car first. Usually she'd be glued to my side to make sure I didn't talk to Darian. She'd been volunteering backstage at the recitals since I was three, and I figured she'd be extra diligent with her duties that night—like she had been at all of our previous recitals since Darian and I had gotten into trouble—to ensure our separation. But she let me go in ahead of her.

I saw Andi as soon as I walked in, and she turned away from me, refusing to make eye contact. I tried to muster up some anger. I wished I could go up to her and say something like, *You narrow-minded traitor.* Anger would have helped take away some of the pain of losing her. But I couldn't be angry with her. All I felt was sadness, and all I could think was, *You were my best friend—can't you see that I need you?*

I took advantage of Mom's delay and went in search of Darian. I found her in one of the dressing rooms, sitting in front of a mirror, putting on makeup. I stood in the doorway.

"You look pretty," I said. "I got you this." I handed her a Godiva dark chocolate bar, her favorite.

"Thanks," she said with a sad smile. "Hey, I brought you something too."

She rummaged around in her bag and pulled out a folded-up *Tulsa World* newspaper story. "I thought you might get something out of this."

It was a two-part story called "Becoming Katie" about a local male-to-female transgender girl. There was a large photo of her, and she was beautiful.

"Thanks. I can't wait to read—"

"There you are," Mom said, appearing out of nowhere. Thank God I was still in the doorway and not in the actual dressing room. I would have been screwed.

"Hi, Ms. Andrews," Darian said meekly.

Mom nodded in Darian's general direction and took me by the arm. "Time to get dressed, Emerald."

I changed into my uniform quickly so I could whip through the article before showtime. It said that Katie had been born Luke, and that she lived relatively close by. Almost everything she said about feeling like she had been born in the wrong body was identical to my own thoughts. One quote hit me really hard:

"It wasn't my fault. It was just nature handing me something that wasn't fair. I couldn't look in the mirror without wanting to cry."

I knew exactly what she meant.

Her mother, a woman named Jazzlyn, came across as supersupportive of Katie's transition. In fact, she seemed awesome. The article said she even took Katie out shopping for girls' clothes.

I looked up at Mom, and for once she wasn't paying attention to what I was doing. She seemed so preoccupied that I probably could have slipped away and found Darian. Instead I followed her eyes and realized that they were glued to all the little girls running around in tutus, and the moms fixing their hair and putting makeup on them.

She's going to need time, I thought.

But I had faith that she'd come around, maybe even become like this woman Jazzlyn. She had to. Or she was going to lose me. I could still scarcely believe that I'd actually had the courage to tell her, and now that I had, there was no going back. I needed her to help me, because I had no one else to turn to. She'd been willing to do so much for me when she'd believed she had a little girl, and I prayed that she'd be just as willing to help me figure out life as her teenage son.

The alternative was too huge and scary to comprehend. I'd read so many heartbreaking stories online about trans kids who came out to their families and were rejected and tossed out onto the street. I didn't think Mom would ever go that far, but I also knew that it would destroy me to live in a home where I was forced to be someone I wasn't. I had to become the person I was supposed to be.

When we all finished our dances and the final curtain fell, I made eye contact with Darian from across the room and held up three fingers. She did the same, and turned around. I knew that she was crying.

On the ride home Mom asked, "Did you decide to tell me that you're transgender tonight because you knew you wouldn't be seeing Darian after this?"

"No," I told her. "I've been doing a lot of research, and I needed to finally get it off my chest. I figured now that summer is coming up, maybe we can start talking about it, without all the pressure of school."

She was silent the rest of the ride home. When we got to the house, I remembered the article about Katie that Darian had given me. I dug it out of my bag and pressed it into her hand.

"Here. Read this," I said. "It might help you understand. This isn't abnormal—there are a lot of other people out there like me."

She glanced down at it and nodded. But on my way up the stairs to my room, I caught her shoving it, unread, into a drawer.

9

I managed to sneak a call to Darian from Susan's house a couple of days later.

"I told Mom," I whispered. "That I'm trans."

"You're kidding me," she said. "Did she freak out? Was it because of the article?"

"No, that's the weird thing. I told her on the ride over before you even gave it to me. I didn't get a chance to tell you before she came into the dressing room. She hasn't brought it up since, though. She just took it in and then didn't respond. I even gave her Katie's story to read when we got home, but I don't think she's looked at it. Thanks for that, by the way."

"Well, I'm damn proud of you," she said. "So what's next?"

"I don't know," I said. "Every day that goes by that Mom doesn't mention it, I get more depressed. She can't see me for who I am. On top of that, school would lynch me if they knew, and I'm not allowed to see you . . ."

I stopped talking, and we sat there in silence for a few minutes.

"Emerald?"

"Yeah."

"You okay?"

"No."

"Talk to me."

I could hear my cousins running through the house around me. Something thumped loudly against a wall, followed by a small crash and several screams, everyone blaming the other for whatever mishap had just occurred.

They all sounded so alive. So normal.

Depression poured over me. Why hadn't Mom brought it up yet? I had thought coming out to her was going to change everything. I knew she'd need time to get used to the idea, but I hadn't considered that who I really was might be *ignored*.

"I don't have a place here anymore," I said slowly. "I don't see the point."

"What do you mean?"

"They all think I'm someone I'm not. And I try to tell them the truth without words, by the way I dress when I'm at home, and by the way I talk, and the things I do. But they still don't see it. It's like being invisible. And now that I've finally admitted it to Mom, it hasn't made a difference. I'm *still* invisible. Stuck inside this . . . *thing*."

I put my hand on one of my breasts, trying to flatten it with my palm while gritting my teeth. I pushed until it hurt, bringing tears to my eyes.

"I hate it," I whispered. "I hate myself. Being alive isn't worth this."

"Emerald . . ."

"I gotta go," I said abruptly, and hung up the phone. I couldn't talk about it anymore. It was too painful. I sucked the tears back in, tried to bury the dark thoughts. But it didn't work. Whatever progress I'd made mentally by joining CAP no longer helped. I retreated back into my head and shut the world out.

Darian was so freaked out by our conversation that she called Susan and told her that I might be suicidal. Susan assumed my depression was because Mom was keeping me apart from Darian, and immediately confronted her. Mom cornered me in return.

"Isn't the Prozac helping?" she asked. "Why didn't you tell me you were feeling this bad?"

"Why would I?" I said dully. "You're the one keeping me away from Darian. And you know that's not the only problem."

She refused to meet my eye, and decided to take me to a new shrink to see if my meds needed adjusting.

The morning of our appointment with the psychiatrist, I dressed in my usual uniform of khaki shorts, a T-shirt, and my hair pulled back in a ponytail, with a bandana around my forehead. We walked into the doctor's office, and I slid down on one side of the couch with my arms crossed, and glared, while Mom sat on the other, her back straight and her purse clutched in her lap.

"Emerald has been really depressed, and I think she needs some help," Mom said.

"Depressed?" the psychiatrist asked, looking at me, then Mom, then me again. I watched him take in my outfit. "Anything in particular that you're depressed about?"

I glared at Mom.

"I'm sensing some tension between the two of you," he prodded gently.

Mom sighed, giving in. "Emerald has a crush on a girl, and I haven't been letting her see her."

"It's not *fair*," I said lamely.

"So you're gay, Emerald?" he asked.

I froze, and then just nodded. There was no way I was telling this stranger that I was trans.

Mom looked like she wanted to bolt toward the door. He turned to her. "And you're not so happy about all of this."

She shook her head.

"I've been exactly where you are," he said kindly. "I have a gay son. And I was not happy about it at all when he came out to me."

She looked at him hopefully.

"But here's the thing," he continued. "That's who he is. There is nothing that I can do to change it. It took me some time to come around, but I'm so happy that I finally did. I took the time to listen to him and see the world through his eyes. He's in his twenties now, and our relationship has never been better. I think what you two need is some family therapy, and I know just the person for it. Would you be willing to work together on this?"

We looked at each other. I nodded, and then she did too. It wasn't a giant breakthrough or anything, but I knew that this doctor had opened a small door for us that had the potential to get us to a better place.

And that's how we met our family therapist, Dr. Benton.

We saw her once a week, alternating between one of us having a thirty-minute session first, and then meeting with her together for the second half hour. But I couldn't tell her I was trans yet either. She was essentially still a stranger, and I felt like I couldn't talk about it with anyone besides Darian. And Mom wasn't able to talk about it with Dr. Benton, because she was still too scared to fully accept it herself. We had reached a stalemate.

"It's okay to come out as gay," Dr. Benton told me during our first session. "But you should also respect that it might take your mom a little bit of time to come around. Don't go blowing the hinges off that closet door."

I didn't see why *I* had to be the one making any concessions, but in our joint sessions Dr. Benton pushed Mom, too. Dr. Benton even convinced Mom that it was good for me to talk to Darian on the phone every now and then, and that it was important for me to be able to interact with other gay teenagers.

Darian was the one who had told me about Openarms Youth Project. She had been hanging out there for some time and encouraged me to join her. They had a Wednesday night dinner with group therapy afterward. Thursdays they hosted a movie or craft night, and every Saturday there was a dance. I left out the detail about the monthly drag shows when I told Mom about OYP.

Darian had told me that there was a church located next door to it, so I really played that fact up when I asked Mom if I could go, thinking that it might make the whole thing somehow seem safer to her. I actually played it up so much that she mistakenly got the impression that OYP was *affiliated* with the church. It's totally not—the church is Baptist, and there's a big fence separating the two structures. But she finally agreed to let me go to one of the Wednesday night dinners as long as Darian didn't go too.

I knew that Mom had another reason for letting me go, aside from Dr. Benton's advice. She was so uncomfortable with Darian that she was willing to set me up with a group of strangers rather than have me spend time alone with Darian. But Darian and I were starting to drift a bit anyway. Never being able to see someone takes its toll. Plus there was suddenly so much change going on between me and Mom that I was distracted and not putting as much effort into trying to talk to Darian as I had before, even though I was now allowed to. She asked me about my distance, so we agreed to meet in secret at OYP my first night there.

We almost got busted. Mom ended up walking in with me, but thankfully Darian hadn't arrived yet. The room was filled with kids who looked nothing like me—lots of emo clothes and haircuts, but I headed straight toward them and introduced myself. Mom marched right up to an older man who was setting up food.

"That's my daughter," I overheard her say as she pointed to me. "She's never been here before."

I cringed a little, but none of the kids seemed to care. A cute girl with supershort blond hair came up to me. "I'm Cassie," she said, oozing confidence. "Why don't you sit with me?"

Another girl named Tanya came up and introduced

herself too. She was blond as well and had hair even shorter than Cassie's. I actually mistook her for a guy at first, and wondered if she might be trans too. She reeked of pot and was obviously stoned out of her mind, but she was funny and self-deprecating in a way that made me feel immediately comfortable around her. As soon as Darian arrived, though, I excused myself and spent the rest of the evening hanging out with her. But something was off between us. We didn't seem to be connecting as strongly, and I was pretty sure it was my fault. My eyes kept wandering around the room, checking everyone out. I couldn't believe that there were this many gay kids in Tulsa. Where had they been hiding this whole time?

I suddenly realized that I'd been staring at Cassie while Darian had been talking to me. Cassie caught me looking and winked. I blushed and quickly turned back to Darian.

"Sorry. What was that?" I asked.

"You should see if your mom will let you come back on Saturdays, to the dance parties. I still can't believe you're actually here."

"Me neither," I said. I snuck a glance back at Cassie. She was still staring.

Mom started letting me go to OYP pretty regularly, but Darian couldn't always make it. She was working a full-time summer job, and I continued to make new casual friends of my own, but I mostly hung around with Cassie and Tanya.

Being around other kids like me over that summer started to make me dread having to return to Lincoln in the fall. Almost everyone I met at OYP was sweet and kind and dedicated to helping others. I was too embarrassed to tell any of them that I went to a Christian school, thinking that they would make fun of me, but the weird thing is that they embodied all of the characteristics that make up the fundamental basis of what Christians are *supposed* to be. Unlike some of the teachers and a lot of the students at Lincoln.

So I started to push back hard once the school year started. I wanted to show everyone at Lincoln that they were wrong in their homophobic beliefs, and I genuinely thought I could help teach them.

Lincoln has something called the Question Box. It's basically exactly what it sounds like—a box where anyone can write down any sort of question and put it inside anonymously, and the Bible study teacher reads the question out loud and gives an answer.

One morning I slipped a piece of paper inside. Later that day in Bible study, the teacher held it up.

"We've got a question here," she said. "And I think it's an important one. It reads: 'What if someone were 100 percent Christian and spent their entire life devoted to only helping others, but they were also gay. Would they still go to hell?'"

Everyone's eyes turned to me, and half the class shot their hands up into the air. The teacher ignored them.

"The answer is yes," she said. "The Bible clearly states that being gay is a sin. And I would suggest that whoever questions this should spend less time trying to help others and try to save themselves first."

I sunk down in my seat, angry and embarrassed. But a few days later I wrote another one.

"'What if a gay person were also a missionary and managed to actually convert hundreds and hundreds of people to Christianity?'" the teacher read. "'Would they still go to hell?'"

She put my piece of paper down and sighed.

"Spreading the word of God is without a doubt one of the most important things we can do as Christians. But if you're not working on being a Christian yourself, it doesn't matter. The gay person would still go to hell when he or she died."

I wrote a few more, pointing out all the weird things people do all the time that the Bible says will send you to hell, like eating pork or wearing clothes with two different kinds of thread. They were ignored, and eventually I just gave up.

The day that I got kicked out of Lincoln was beautiful.

I mean the actual day itself, not the event. It was unseasonably warm and sunny for October, but mentally it was the darkest day of my life up until that point.

I didn't even know it was happening until it was all over; my mom had to fill me in. She told me that the vice principal had called her the day before and asked her to come for a meeting that Friday. They pulled out all the letters I'd written for the Question Box about the Bible's contradictions when it came to homosexuality, and put them on the desk in front of her, using them as proof that I was gay myself, even though the notes were supposed to have been anonymous. The vice principal also said another student had claimed that I'd confessed that I was gay, and that homosexuality was a violation of their honor code and grounds for immediate expulsion. They made her feel like she was the worst mother on earth, that it was all her fault.

When school let out that day, she was waiting for me. I got into the car and knew immediately that something was wrong. I could feel it emanating off her. As we pulled out of the parking lot, she kept her eyes straight ahead and said, "They've asked you to leave. That was your last day at Lincoln."

"Huh?" I asked, confused. "Like, right now? What about my locker?" For some reason that was all that registered at first.

"They'll pack it up and send it in a box."

The reality refused to settle in. I had just ordered my letter jacket for track. I was training for another state run later in the year. *But I was a Spotlight Student of the Year,* I thought stupidly. Never mind that they were actually right about my violating their twisted honor code, but it was the fact that I had dared to even *ask questions* that they'd used as the foundation for the expulsion.

This was not what Jesus was about. I knew it in my heart. Every single one of his teachings was based on love and acceptance. And this massive organization that claimed to do all of its work in his name was throwing me to the curb because of who I was. None of it made sense.

The only thing that did make sense was that this was the last rejection of myself that I could take. It was clear to me that I was worthless. A disgusting degenerate that wasn't fit to be around other people. All of the mental progress I'd made going to OYP, and in my weekly therapy meetings with Mom, vanished.

The sun's cheeriness felt like it was mocking me. The

world outside was shiny and normal, but the inside of the car had never been darker. When we pulled into our driveway, I got out and walked quickly ahead of Mom. As I passed through the kitchen, I grabbed a butcher knife out of the drawer and went to my room. I tore off my uniform, that disgusting plaid skirt, and hurled it into a corner. I considered taking it out back and burning it, and for a moment I felt happy, realizing I'd never have to wear it again.

From downstairs I heard the sound of Mom's bedroom door shutting, and the second of joy passed. I threw my shirt into the same corner and pulled on some sweatpants and a baggy sweater. The full realization of what had just happened finally began to sink in. I looked at the knife, and light from the window flashed off it, blinding me for a second. And then I remembered that I *did* still have a place that accepted me. The Civil Air Patrol.

I shoved the knife under my pillow, ran downstairs, and pounded on Mom's door, telling her that I wanted to go to practice that day.

"Fine," she said from inside, her voice sounding a million miles way.

When I arrived at practice, I told everyone that I'd been kicked out because the school thought I was too masculine. They just laughed—being overly masculine was a good thing there. Even if they had any suspicions of their own about my being gay (transgender wasn't even on their radar), I knew it didn't matter. They told me not to worry about it, that everything would be okay, and we practiced our drills like it was any other day.

Dad was waiting for me afterward. I assumed that Mom had sent him because she couldn't even look at me anymore. But he was there for a different reason. We drove back toward his house as he rambled on about sports, but he suddenly pulled off the main road and stopped in front of a dingy-looking stadium with a big painted sign at the top of the bleachers that read, CATOOSA INDIANS.

"Welcome to your new school!" he said.

I looked at him like he was crazy.

"Too soon, Dad," I said. "I *just* got kicked out."

"I know, but now you'll be closer to me. You can come over after school."

He was just trying to help, but the idea of starting over again at a new school so fast was too much. I might not have been happy at Lincoln, but it was the only thing I knew. I'd been going there almost my entire life. I suddenly felt chilly. Freezing, in fact. I began to shiver violently, and asked him to turn up the heat and take me home.

As soon as he dropped me off, I changed back into sweatpants and locked myself in my bedroom. I curled up on the bed and reached my hand under the pillow.

The knife was cold, but solid. Comforting. I held it to my wrist and gave an experimental push. It left a faint red line in my skin. I tried sawing back and forth a little. It felt right.

I called Darian, not caring if Mom caught me. She picked up almost immediately. I explained what had happened, but she didn't get the full impact that it was having on me right away.

"This is a *good* thing," she said. "That place was horrible."

"But it's not about the school," I said. "This is about me—I am worthless."

I started sobbing, and she comforted me, saying all the right things, like how soon everyone would get to know the real me, and that they would love me. That no one would judge. But I couldn't hear it. All I felt was a rejection so deep and extreme that it cut to the soul, and I wanted it to end. I pushed the knife harder onto my wrist, and watched my pumping artery push the skin up against the blade, as if the blood *wanted* to be let out. I could barely hear Darian anymore; there was a rushing sound in my ears. I was going to hell anyway. I might as well speed up the trip. Or maybe I'd actually meet God, and I could finally ask him why so many of the people who follow him are so evil. We'd have a real man-to-man.

A flash of something Darian was saying suddenly shot through my thoughts. ". . . and you're stronger than them," she said. "You have to know that."

If I killed myself, then the assholes at Lincoln would win.

"I have a knife," I said.

"Then get rid of it *right now*," she said.

I knocked it off the side of the bed, heard the handle thud on the carpet.

"I don't know how to do this," I whispered.

"You won't be alone," she promised.

We stayed on the phone until the sun came up, and I passed out immediately after we said our final "I love you."

I slept late the next morning, and when I went downstairs, I found Mom in her bedroom, staring at the television.

She moved aside a little, and I stretched out next to her. We barely spoke the entire day, attempting to adjust to our new reality under the numbing effects of reality television.

The next day was more of the same, and on the third day I was lying on my bed staring at the ceiling when Mom came in and sat down beside me. She saw the knife, still on my floor, and picked it up.

"This trans stuff is real, isn't it?" she asked. "It's not going away. You're not going to grow out of it."

"No, I'm not."

"But how are you going to live like this?"

"When you ignore the fact that this is who I am, it makes me think that life isn't worth living *at all* sometimes."

She looked at me, and then glanced back down at the knife.

"You really would have done this?" she asked.

"I tried."

She nodded, and tears started streaming down her cheeks, down her neck. "I will support you. I can't lose you."

"You won't," I said. "I'm still me. I'll always still be me. But I need my body to be my own."

She nodded again. And I knew that she finally got it.

10

I started attending Catoosa High, and it was pretty much the polar opposite of Lincoln. The classes were cake. It was prime deer hunting season, and teachers and kids alike were constantly skipping to head out into the woods. One day in history class our teacher just showed us a movie about how to gut a stag.

I made a few casual friends, mostly the misfit stoner kids, along with Alyssa and my future prom date, Jessica. I wore whatever I wanted, which meant loose shirts, jeans, and either a headband or a hat to hide my hair. People constantly yelled out to me in the halls, asking if I was a boy or a girl. A guy randomly came up to me and said, "I'd punch you if you weren't actually a girl."

"Whatever," I mumbled.

One day I went to use the bathroom, and when I walked inside, a girl freaked out.

"You aren't supposed to be in here!" she screamed. "Get out!"

I ignored her and slammed the stall door in her face.

I don't want to be here either, bitch, I thought as I sat down.

"No, it's okay. That's a girl," I heard someone whisper.

Nope.

We were still in therapy with Dr. Benton, and at our first appointment right after I started at Catoosa, Mom just blurted it out.

"Emerald is transgender," she said, and hearing it finally come out of her mouth, spoken as a truth that she believed, was almost surreal.

"Yes, well, I'm not exactly surprised, to be honest," Dr. Benton said. "The signs were all there. It's not really my area of expertise, but there's actually another therapist in the building who specializes in this."

His name was Taylor Burns, and Mom called him as soon as we got to the car.

"Hi, yes," she said, leaving a message. "I have a daughter who is transgender, and we'd really love to make an appointment to speak with you."

She hadn't called me her son, but she'd at least said the word "transgender" again. I beamed.

"Can we go cut my hair off now?" I asked.

"One thing at a time, Emerald," she said. "One thing at a time."

I could live with that. Because I finally felt as though I were going to be able to *start* living.

My heart was pounding before my first appointment with our new therapist, and I couldn't stop fidgeting with the buttons on my shirt. Everything in my life was moving so fast. Just a few days before, I'd been willing to let go of it all, I had been so close to wanting to leave this world, and now that everything had completely turned around, I didn't want the momentum to stop. I even followed in Darian's steps and quit dance, so that I could focus all my energy on this new phase of my life. Just because Dr. Benton had suggested Taylor Burns didn't mean he'd necessarily be the right fit for me, but since he specialized in gender dysphoria—the medical term for people like me who know that they were born into a body that doesn't match their gender identity—I knew that he could be the one to set me on the road to physically becoming a man.

After I'd first discovered Skylarkeleven's videos, I'd memorized all the initial basic steps I'd have to take: I would need to live publicly as a guy for one full year before I would be allowed to get any sort of surgery, and I'd have to have that period documented by a gender therapist like Taylor Burns. During that time, if he agreed in his professional opinion that I was indeed transgender, he could write a recommendation to a doctor for me to start hormone replacement therapy in the form of regular testosterone injections, which would deepen my voice, stop my periods, increase muscle definition, and help me grow facial hair (among other things, but I will get into that later). After my year was up, I could start reviewing my surgery options with Mom—since I was still a minor, I'd need her permission. But at my first appointment with the new therapist, getting him to agree that I should be on testosterone was my main focus.

It's really important to be clear that this was *my* particular plan for transitioning. It's not necessarily the same path that every trans man takes. Some get top surgery before starting on testosterone (or "T," as it's often called), some *can't* take T due to intolerance. Some don't get any surgery at all. I was following the basic guidelines that doctors and gender therapists have mapped out for transgender people, but transitioning is a deeply personal and individual process that can take any number of different roads.

For my first appointment I wore jeans, a red-and-black-checkered flannel, and a wool cap pulled down low on my head. I'd realized that with my hair just down to my shoulders now, I didn't even have to pull it back all the time to look like a boy. If I wore a hat over it, I looked like any other normal skater guy with long hair. In fact, I was passing as male a lot of the time now whenever I was out in public. I could change in the guys' dressing room at the mall, and no one would even blink.

"You look like a stoner," Mom told me in the car on the way over.

I ignored her. I was too nervous to start a fight.

We sat in the waiting room until the office door opened and the therapist ushered us in. He had short hair, glasses, a round face, and a beard. I'd been calling him Mr. Burns in my head, so I'd been half-expecting someone like the hunched-over old man from *The Simpsons*.

"Call me Taylor," he said, gesturing toward a small couch. His office looked like someone's living room—in addition to the plush brown sofa, there was a matching armchair and ottoman, and a fancier-looking chair with a throw blanket draped over the back, which he sat in.

"So, what are you here for?" he asked.

Since he was getting straight to the point, I figured I should as well.

"I'm transgender," I said. "And I want to cut my hair, change my name, start testosterone, and get top surgery."

He didn't seem fazed at all. "Okay," he said, as if these were all totally normal things to say. He then asked Mom if he could speak to me alone and she went back to the lobby. "How long have you felt this way?" he asked after she closed the door.

I talked nonstop for an entire hour. He nodded a lot, jotted down notes, and was warm and encouraging. I felt totally at ease with him. I knew I'd found my guy, and he proved it when he called Mom back in at the end of the session.

"You have a very nice young man here," Taylor said.

I watched Mom's eyes shoot straight to my hair.

He explained to her that he would likely end up recommending testosterone, but since I was only fifteen, we'd need her permission.

"I'd like to have some more sessions before I'm willing to do that," she said.

I was bummed, but it wasn't like I'd been expecting her to automatically say yes. I knew that it was unrealistic for her to jump right on the T-train with me, and Taylor agreed that more sessions were necessary anyway. Since the holidays were about to hit, we made our next appointment for early January. He explained that from that point forward he'd spend time with us both alone and together during our meetings.

After this first taste of victory, I was tempted to go ahead and cut off all my hair as soon as I got back to my bedroom. But on the drive home I listened to Mom talk about how she liked Taylor, and I realized that this wasn't going to be the same journey if I didn't have her support. She was the only member of my family who knew what was going on, and she was so close to fully coming around. I could feel it, and if I acted out now, it would set us back so far. It wasn't worth the risk.

Christmas was rough that year. After such an awesome first meeting with Taylor, it felt weird to have to go right back into the closet about my gender. And since I was already partially passing as male in public (almost every shop clerk or waiter I encountered called me "sir" based on my looks), it was bizarre to have all the people who supposedly knew and loved me the most keep calling me "she." When it came time to open presents at Papa and Gigi's house, Gigi said, "Okay, all the girls go to the tree and open your gifts first!"

I shot Mom a desperate look. She gave me a sympathetic smile but nodded toward the tree, motioning for me to get down on the floor with all my female cousins.

"Why don't you *dress* like a girl?" Wes yelled at me from the sofa. I told him to shut up, even though I'm sure he was just annoyed that I got to open presents before him. I skulked over to the pile of gifts and grabbed one with my name on it, hating that I felt so ungrateful.

It was from Gigi, and it was a new knife, a thick,

heavy-duty folding model with a beautiful wooden handle. I flipped it over in my hand, appreciating the heft, and saw that it had "Emerald" engraved in huge letters on the wooden part. It was *almost* the perfect present.

The absolute best gift I got that year arrived in the mail the day after Christmas. It was from Darian's cousin's fiancé, the trans guy. She'd told him all about me, and he sent me a binder—a tight piece of fabric worn over your chest in place of a bra—that flattens your breasts. I opened the box up in front of Mom and pulled out the white ring of elastic.

"It looks awfully small," she said doubtfully.

"That's the whole point," I said, running upstairs. I reached my arms up and through it and pulled it down over my chest, maneuvering it into place. It *hurt*, and even made it a little hard to breathe. But as soon as I slipped a shirt over it, the effect was seamless. It was like there was nothing there. Even when I stood up straight, with my shoulders all the way back. I ran back downstairs to show Mom.

"It's like they're totally gone," I crowed. "PLEASE can I get my hair cut now? *Please?*"

She stared at my chest for a moment before meeting my eyes. "Not yet," she said. "I'm still not ready."

A few days later I went shopping with Gigi, Mom, and a few of my cousins. I loaded up my arms with flannel shirts and had started to head toward the men's changing room, when I felt a hand on my arm.

"Nope," Mom said. "Not with the rest of the family around. Not yet." She pointed toward the women's changing rooms.

I felt like I was stuck, and I couldn't wait for our next appointment with Taylor. The changes were happening right in front of her eyes, but she was still resisting the inevitable. I was trying to be patient, but I couldn't figure out what was holding her back. There was some last piece of this puzzle that went beyond the idea of her losing her daughter, and I didn't know how to solve it.

I called her on it during our next therapy appointment. "You know that this is happening," I said. "And you're being as supportive as you think you can be, and I appreciate it. I really, really do. But how long is it going to take before you can fully accept this? And why is my hair the biggest issue that you seem to have?"

Taylor didn't prod. We waited for her to speak. She was staring at her knees and looking like she was doing everything in her power to keep from crying.

She finally looked up at me. "The binder is fine because I know your breasts are still there. I can even get behind the idea of the testosterone, but that's because I think it's something that will initially be mostly invisible. But the hair is external. I've seen what you look like with your hair pulled back, and you're right, I can see a boy in there. And I know that once you take that step, it's one that I won't be able to tune out. There's no going back. I won't be able to pretend anymore."

"Pretend *what*?" I said, my voicing getting louder. "I'm a *guy*! And I'm trapped!"

"I know that," she said. "I don't doubt it at all anymore. What I'm having trouble with is understanding how this all fits into the world. What your place is in the natural order of things."

That stopped me short. "Are you talking about the Bible?" I asked.

"I guess that, too," she said. "But I mean in the even bigger sense. Why, or how, does this even happen?"

I'd asked myself that a million times and had never been able to come up with a remotely decent answer, except for it being some sort of cruel genetic hiccup, or some weird endurance test that God was putting me through.

"Are either of you familiar with the term 'Two-Spirit'?" Taylor asked.

Mom and I glanced at each other and shook our heads.

"In Native American culture someone who doesn't conform to the gender identity they were born into is called Two-Spirit. Since they exhibit both male and female characteristics, they are believed to have the spirits of both a man and a woman. And since they have been gifted with the ability to see the world through both a male and female perspective, they are believed to be incredibly wise. Traditionally they would often become spiritual leaders or healers."

We have a little Native American blood in us and have always embraced that distant tie, but it was the first time we had ever heard of Two-Spirit, and it hit a really strong chord with both of us. We were quiet on the way home, and I couldn't stop thinking about how the sense of time and history involved gave us proof that what was happening to me had been going on in others since humans had first existed.

It turned out that Mom was thinking the same thing.

"It just makes so much more sense to me now," she told me that night while I helped her chop up some vegetables for dinner. "What he said about Two-Spirits often being healers. I mean, look at how you healed Bambi."

Bambi was a baby flying squirrel I'd found the previous spring in the mouth of one of the cats that lived in our back woods. I had managed to wrestle him free, and Mom helped me nurse him back to health. I named him after the Disney orphan, and soon he was gliding from the cabinets to the floor and driving all the dogs crazy. Of all the broken animals that had ever come to stay with us, he was the best. In a weird way I wished I were like that little creature—a mammal that could soar. I couldn't help but relate while watching him gain strength and learn how to use his body.

At our next appointment the following week, Mom was visibly more relaxed, and it turned out that she had fully opened her mind at the perfect time.

"The Equality Center has asked me to start up a teen transgender support group at their headquarters," Taylor told us. "I'd love it if the two of you would join. I really think it would help strengthen your relationship."

I looked at Mom hopefully.

"Okay," she said. "I think I'd like that."

11

I'd heard of the place before, but it was the first time I'd gone to the Dennis R. Neill Equality Center. It's located on a remote corner of downtown Tulsa, and they offer tons of different kinds of support to the LGBT community—everything from legal services to HIV testing to yoga to AA meetings. They even have their own lending library and a gay pride gift store.

The first thing I noticed when I walked in was how clean and fresh it smelled. Like some kind of gently scented soap, friendly and safe. And the volunteers at the front desk were immediately welcoming. They showed us the way to one of the meeting rooms on the second floor. We were the last to arrive, and I froze for a moment at the door. It was a group for all trans teens, but at that moment every single person there happened to be a trans guy. I couldn't believe there were this many in our area. And even though I was wearing my normal boy outfit of jeans, a plaid shirt, and a baseball cap with my hair down, the difference was staggering. These dudes all looked like they had transitioned long ago, and almost all of them had facial hair.

I hunched my shoulders over and stomped to the table, pulled out a chair, and sat with my legs extra wide. "Hey. I'm Emerald," I mumbled in what was possibly the deepest voice I'd ever used up to that point.

I had to overcompensate, because not only was I the only one who could still potentially be mistaken for a girl, but I was also the youngest in the group by at least five years.

But everyone quickly made me feel at ease. We went around the table, and everyone had a chance to talk about something that they were struggling with. When I'd walked in, I hadn't been able to fathom these guys having anything to complain about—they were all exactly what I was aspiring to be. But of course life is so much more complicated than that, and each of them had something painful or troubling that was going on, and everyone in the room was so kind and offered helpful advice to one another.

When it was my turn, I was still a little too overwhelmed to say much aside from the fact that I knew I was a trans man and had just started the process of transitioning. Mom squeezed my hand under the table when I was done. Almost everyone in the group came up to me afterward and congratulated me on starting out, and Mom, too, for being there to support me. As much as the experience meant personally, I knew it was important for *her* to get the reassurance that there was a community out there for me.

I bought a small plastic rainbow bracelet from the gift shop on my way out, and when we got to our car in the parking lot, one of the guys from the group, a man named Danny, stopped us.

"I don't think you understand what a big deal it is that you're here," he said to Mom. She blushed.

"No, seriously," he said. "It's really rare to have parents that are so on board. Mine sure as hell weren't."

"To be fair, it's taken me a while to come around," Mom said.

He nodded. "Totally understandable, but you *did*. That's what counts."

We ended up talking with him there in the lot for almost an hour, about how we'd gotten to where we were, and what things had been like for me as a kid.

"By the way," he said as we were finishing up and saying our good-byes, "I'm not sure if you realize this, but you totally pass as a guy already."

"Seriously?" I asked, grinning. "You mean it? Even with the long hair?" I shot Mom a look.

"Even with the long hair," he confirmed.

"That went well," Mom said when we finally got into the car.

I nodded. I could still smell the scent of the Equality Center on me, and I realized it was coming from the bracelet I'd just bought. I lifted my wrist up to my nose and held it there, letting the faint fragrance envelop me, making me feel warm and accepted.

About a week later Mom let me get another haircut. She still wasn't ready for the full boy cut, but she let me get it done all shaggy and down just below my ears, like Shane, my favorite character from *The L Word*. She was such a chick magnet on that show, I figured I couldn't go wrong.

We also started having much more serious discussions about testosterone.

"Well," she said, "I suppose it would be easier to transition in high school than it would be once you're out in the work field. Better to have your life already started, once you're ready to actually start your life."

"Yes," I agreed immediately. "You are absolutely right."

"I'll keep thinking about it," she said.

I started working out a ton, trying to get abs and build up my arms, in preparation for the day when she would finally relent. I wanted to get a head start on my body so that once the changes started, I'd already be at a point to make the most of the improved muscle development that can come with taking testosterone. I'd been doing tons of research on it, and even put together a whole notebook for my mom, full of facts and info on the effects of testosterone, with tabs that divided up certain topics, like proper injection techniques and common myths—such as that it would turn me into a raging monster.

And just a few weeks later, for my sixteenth birthday, she finally relented and said that I could cut my hair short, the way I wanted.

I went back to Spalon and watched in the mirror as the final inches were cut away. And there I was. Me, for the first time ever, staring back.

• • •

Mom took me to an Italian restaurant for dinner to celebrate, one of those places with large sheets of paper covering the table and a cup of crayons to draw with.

"It's time we pick out your new name," she said after we'd ordered. "I've been think about it a lot, and I've got a great idea. Why don't you call yourself Emeril? You know, like Emeril Lagasse! It *sounds* like 'Emerald,' and so that way people won't have such a hard time with the change!"

She beamed, clearly proud of herself.

"No way," I said. "First of all, who wants to be named after Emeril Lagasse? And second, no one would actually call me that. They'd just keep saying 'Emerald' because it's basically the exact same name but with a *d* sound at the end."

Her face fell, and I felt bad. As exciting as this all was for me, I had to grant her some leeway. The name she'd given me was so specific. "Emerald" meant so much to her.

I grabbed a red crayon out of the cup. "What if we play around with my middle name?" I said, and wrote out "Ariana." "I know I don't want it to be something random, like Jay. It should be meaningful."

"I like that idea," she said with a smile. She wrote it on the table too and squinted.

"What if we just dropped the *a* and made it 'Arian'?" she asked.

"Arian," I said out loud, trying it out.

It had a familiar ring, but I couldn't place it. I liked it. "Arian," I said aloud again.

"Arian," she echoed. "I could get used to that, easy!"

"I wonder if there is anyone else with that name," I said,

pulling out my phone. "I feel like I've heard it before, but I can't think of anyone."

"Arianism" popped up in my browser. "Wait," I said. "It means 'a belief that Jesus isn't a divine being.' It's considered heresy." I scrolled down a little farther and saw the word "Aryan" pop up.

"Oh, right," I said, mortified. "It also sounds exactly like the word for Hitler's idea of the perfect race."

"Yeah, that's not going to work," Mom said. We crossed it out.

"What if we just drop another *a* and make it 'Arin'?" I said, drawing a line through the fourth letter.

"Arin," she said.

"Arin," I repeated, feeling it click in my brain. That was the one.

In my family I ended up having to come out as trans only to my cousins. I found out from Mom that she had told Papa and Gigi the week after I'd gotten kicked out of Lincoln. She told me that she had been terrified about their reaction, but they had been incredibly calm and unfazed. They'd told her that since I was her child, they all had to love and support me no matter what. I'd always loved them so much, and hearing that just about made my heart burst.

Susan already knew too, since she and Mom are so close, and she was immediately on board. Mom wanted to explain it to Wes herself since he was younger. He had a hard time with it.

"Why can't you just be a normal sister?" he kept asking me after Mom broke the news.

"Because I'm not a girl," I'd say, and he'd continue to sulk. He was unhappy about it, but he didn't tease me about it or anything. It was more that he started to avoid me. In a lot of ways I still considered him my annoying little brother, though, so it was sort of a relief. He was the least of my worries as far as family acceptance went; I figured that he was young enough to have plenty of time to get used to the idea.

By the time we told Dad, more than anything else he was upset by the fact that he was the last to know.

"I can't believe this has been going on this whole time behind my back," he grouched. "Why didn't anyone tell me?"

"Probably because when you found out about Darian, you said that I was too pretty to be a lesbian," I said. "That didn't really set up lot of confidence about your reaction to this."

He was weirded out for a while, but things went back to normal between us pretty fast.

I told all my cousins in person. Amanda was uncomfortable with it at first, but Cheyenne just said, "Oh, please. I've known that since you were a kid."

Before I even had a chance to say anything to Dewayne, he came up to me, punched me on the shoulder, and said, "What's up, dude?" before wandering off again. And that was that.

My new name caught on immediately with everyone, as if it were what they'd always called me. Pronouns remained an issue for a while, especially among members of my dad's side of the family. They slipped up and kept referring to me as "she" for a long time. But they eventually got the hang of it.

I quit CAP so I could put all my energy into transitioning, but I stayed close with Jon and Samuel and a few others. None of them had any problem with me changing my gender. I started telling my few friends at school, like Alyssa and Jessica, to call me Arin. They accepted it too (with the exception of Jessica's occasional grumblings). Mom and I worked it out with the principal that I could use the nurse's bathroom so I didn't make any of the girls uncomfortable. I didn't want to put myself at risk by using the guys' room. And besides, the one time a friend took me in there, I wasn't too impressed. It reeked, and the urinals were full of chewing tobacco wads. But at least there weren't bloody tampons in boxes next to all the toilets, so that was a step up.

It was shocking to me how cool the school administration was. There's an old joke in Tulsa that we don't just live in the Bible Belt; we live in the *buckle* of the Bible Belt. And that tends to come with a lot of intolerance. I knew how incredibly lucky I was to have it all happen so fast and so easily. In the trans teen support group and at OYP, I'd heard plenty of horror stories about kids being rejected by their families after coming out as trans or gay. Repeating any of those stories here would be a breach of confidentiality and the safe space these support groups create, but 41 percent of transgender people attempt suicide at least one time in their life, which is around twenty-five times the national average. And I'm still haunted by the movie *Boys Don't Cry*, which is based on the story of Brandon Teena, a trans man who was raped and murdered in Nebraska in the early 1990s. (If you've never seen it, watch it the second you're done with this book.)

I made a pact with myself that I wouldn't take for granted the acceptance I received, that if there were ever anyone who needed support or guidance with their own transition, I would do everything I could to help them. I wanted to inspire other trans kids, the way that Katie Hill, the girl from the *Tulsa World* article, had. And I wanted to educate cis people about trans rights too. When I mentioned this to Taylor in one of our therapy meetings, he asked if I'd be willing to sit in on a panel discussion at one of the local colleges.

"It's for a sociology class," he explained. "The professor is looking for a few trans people to talk about their experiences, as well as their family members. Would you be interested?"

The idea of talking in front of a group of strangers was terrifying, but I wanted to stick to my new advocacy resolve, so I said yes.

Despite feeling like I might pass out in fear when I first sat down in front of thirty-five older college students, the night went off without a hitch. Mom came with me, and we both spoke for about fifteen minutes about my life experiences so far. There was another woman on the panel, pretty with long dark hair, and when she introduced herself, the name sounded oddly familiar. *Jazzlyn.* As she started talking, I realized that it was Katie Hill's mother! I was too starstruck to say anything to her after, so my mom introduced us. It turns out that they'd already met at a support group for parents of trans teens that Mom had started going to.

"The *Tulsa World* story about Katie really helped me a lot," I said shyly.

"I'm happy to hear that," she said, giving me a little hug.

"And I know my daughter would be happy to hear that too."

I had no idea that Katie would soon become one of the most important people in my entire life.

A few weeks later Mom and I went to the trans support group, but it was a smaller crowd than normal that night. I tended to like those meetings better. It felt more intimate, and everyone got a little bit more time to talk about whatever it was they needed help with.

We were going around and saying our names, when suddenly the door flew open and a girl walked in. Her dark hair covered her face at first.

"Sorry," she murmured as she sat down in an empty chair across the table from me. She looked up finally, and I felt my heart drop. It was *her*. Katie Hill. When it was my turn to talk, I rambled on about school, too distracted by how pretty she was in person to even really know what I was saying.

After the meeting I introduced myself.

"That story that ran in *Tulsa World* was amazing," I said. "It really helped me feel like I wasn't alone."

"Thanks," she said, smiling faintly. "I'm really glad to hear that."

"I'm hoping that my gender therapist lets me start on T soon. It's killing me that I haven't yet."

"I'm sure he'll sign off before too long," she said. "You seem like you're in a really good place. Listen, I gotta run. I'm exhausted. It was really nice meeting you."

• • •

I was excited to tell Darian that I had met the girl from the article she had given me. We still sometimes met up at OYP when she was able to get the time off from work, but we had continued to drift further and further apart. I still struggled with her lesbian identity and what it said about us. I wanted to be with a girl who wanted a guy. Plus I was totally caught up in my new life as an out trans man and getting to mingle with entire groups of other trans and gay teens for the first time in my life. All sorts of new social opportunities were opening up. I started hanging out with Tanya a lot, the person I'd met on my very first night at OYP. And just like I had originally expected, Tanya eventually began to transition and go by the name Dale. I was so excited to help him, especially since he was too scared to tell his family.

"They will never understand," he told me one night at OYP. "It's really starting to mess with my head, being Dale out in the world but still Tanya at home."

"Give it a little time," I said. "I never thought my mom would come around either."

He didn't look very hopeful. "I think our mothers are two very different people," he said, before wandering off to say hi to another friend. Cassie suddenly appeared beside me.

"Nice haircut, Cassie," I said. It was even shorter than it had been the first time we'd met.

"It's Carl now," he said.

"No way! That's awesome! Since when?"

"I've always known I'm trans. It just took a while for me to get my shit together and actually deal with it."

He said it like transitioning was no big thing, as if it had been as easy as flipping a switch. He seemed so cocky and confident, and I felt myself blush a little. I was a little bit in awe of him. Plus, he was even cuter now than when he had been Cassie. I suddenly couldn't stop staring at his lips.

"I gotta take off. You want to walk me to my car?" he asked, bumping his shoulder against my arm and then hopping back slightly.

"Um, I-I guess," I stammered. I rolled back and forth on the balls of my feet nervously. *Why does he want me to walk him to his car?* I wondered.

He stepped toward me again with a wicked little grin, and I could feel his breath on my face. It smelled like wintergreen gum. "Will you kiss me there?" he asked.

Oh, that's why.

I blushed and felt my whole body tingle. "U-um . . . ," I stuttered, but suddenly he stood on his toes and flung his arms around my neck, and we were making out. The entire room fell away and went silent in my brain for a few seconds, until my conscience kicked in and I became acutely aware of every sound around us. The thumping music and shouting of other kids became hyper-amplified, and I felt like a spotlight from the dance floor was suddenly pointed directly at us. I pulled away and looked around anxiously, my face burning.

"Oh, relax," he said. "No one is paying any attention."

"I should go," I said, and backed away slowly. I was terrified that someone who knew Darian had seen us. Even though I'd been pulling away from Darian emotionally, she was still my girlfriend. And I never in a million years had imagined myself as someone who would cheat. But I'd just done exactly that.

I got a call from Darian the next day, and before I even picked up, I knew that she knew. She was sniffling when I answered.

"One of my friends saw you making out last night. Is it true?"

"Um, no?" I said timidly. I felt like such an asshole for lying, especially since it was obvious that I was. But she was so hurt that I clammed up. I didn't want her to cry or feel bad, and my flawed logic told me that denying what I'd done would keep that from happening.

"But they *saw* you two together," she said.

"I mean, he gave me a big hug good-bye when he left." The words came flying out of my mouth before I even knew what they would be. *Tell the truth,* I told myself. But I couldn't. I was already trapped in the lie.

Somehow I got Darian to believe that her friend was mistaken and that everything was fine between us. But just a couple of weeks later, I ended up making out with Carl again. And once more I got busted by one of Darian's friends.

I think by then a part of me was hoping I'd get caught. I hated the feeling of being a liar, especially since I was now revealing so many truths in my life. Emotionally it felt like a huge step backward.

I still feel terrible about the way I handled it.

"Is it because you're not attracted to me anymore?" Darian sobbed over the phone when she called.

My messed-up teenage brain logic took over again. That

seemed like a good excuse to use; it was much less complicated than getting into all my reservations about how she
identified solely as a lesbian and how that confused *me* about
who *I* was. I was too young to realize just how fluid sexuality
can be, even though I was starting to understand that I was
probably kind of bisexual. Kissing Carl had been really fun,
not to mention that I was suddenly living an entirely new
existence, one that I could actually engage in. My relationship with Darian had been built mainly on letters and dis-
creet phone calls. And while that had made it so intense and
authentic, it had been almost entirely based on an emotional
response as opposed to a physical one. I knew that it was
time to move on. Still, I should have had more integrity than
to use her insecurity as an easy way out. It was stupid and
immature, and I still apologize to her about it whenever we
talk now. To this day, I hate thinking about what I said next:

"Yeah, I guess I'm just not into your body," I agreed. "I
can't do this anymore." Those last words sounded familiar as
they came out of my mouth, and I realized with shame that
it was the exact same thing that Andi had texted when she'd
friend-dumped me.

"Fine, Arin," Darian said, suddenly cold. "I can't either.
Good luck, with everything."

I felt miserable, but also relieved that it was over. I knew
that it was finally time to try the new me out in the world,
in a place where no one knew that Emerald had ever even
existed.

12

I got my first real chance that March, when Mom decided to take Wes and me on a cruise for our spring break. It would be the first time I got to completely immerse myself in an environment solely as Arin. Mom took me shopping for boys' swimwear and a suit to wear for the formal nights. "There's one more thing I'm going to need," I said once we got home.

"Yeah, what's that?" she asked, looking up from her computer.

"A packer."

"One of those fake penises you put in your underwear?"

"Yeah. If I'm going to be walking around in a guy's bathing suit, it needs to look like there's something in there."

She didn't bat an eye. "Okay. Then let's get you a penis."

I sat next to her at the computer and showed her the one I'd been researching. It was from a company called Peecock that offered three different sizes of prosthetic penises with testicles, which attached to a cup that fitted around the entire vagina. The penises came with a special funnel-shaped insert that you could take out and clean, so that they served as an STP (stand-to-pee) device as well—a much more evolved version of my childhood canister lid funnel.

"What size should I get?" I asked.

They came in three lengths, and the descriptions were as follows:

Four inches: "It takes no time to master peeing with it. . . . Remember as they always say, less is more!"

Five and a half inches: "The efficient all-rounder."

Six and a half inches: "'Handsome' in appearance and almost majestic like! . . . For those who love to strut around proudly with a big bulge!"

"That one," I said immediately, pointing to the six and a half.

"Arin, that's going to look ridiculous down your pants," Mom said. "You're just looking for a bulge, and with your frame, the four-inch is going to be fine. Consider it your starter penis. Besides, it says it's easier to pee through when you're first learning."

I couldn't bring myself to tell her that I'd pretty much mastered peeing standing up before the fifth grade, so I agreed, silently planning on an upgrade at some point.

Ten days later Mom was fixing lunch when I went to check the front porch for any "packages."

"Let me feel," she said when I took it out of the box, and she grabbed it from my hands. "Oooh, it's squishier than I thought it would be," she said.

"Give it," I said, snatching it back.

I ran upstairs and thoroughly washed it off and dried it before taking off my jeans and underwear and holding it up to myself.

The skin tone was off, and it was obviously not real, but I still felt euphoric seeing it between my legs. I squinted my eyes a little so that everything was slightly blurry, and that was even better—it didn't look as fake that way. My body was finally morphing into the one that I'd seen in my dreams.

I gave it a little shake with my hand to see it swing back and forth, and silently cursed myself for not fighting for the larger model. *Still, it's literally better than nothing,* I thought.

I pulled on a pair of tight boxer briefs and stuck it inside those. Then it really looked real. I put my jeans back on and ran back downstairs to the kitchen.

"Well?" I asked proudly. "What do you think?"

Mom burst out laughing. "Why is it sticking down your pant leg like that? You look like you're going to a party with a rolled-up sock taped to your thigh."

I looked down, failing to see the problem. I liked it. "What's wrong?" I asked. "How else are people going to know I have one?"

"You should be subtle about it," Mom said. "No woman wants to see the goods up front. Leave a little mystery."

She reached down and started to adjust it through my jeans. "Put it in the *middle*," she said.

"I thought it looked weird that way, though," I said, swatting her hand away. "Let me do it." I reached down my pants and put the shaft in the center.

"Hmm, yeah, that looks better," she said, cupping her chin in one hand and tilting her head.

Peeing through it while standing up was pretty easy, but it still required a little bit of rearranging first, since the cup tended to move around in my underwear, and I needed to make sure it was pushed tight around my vagina so nothing would spill. So whenever I used the men's room when I was out in public, I made sure to go into a stall so that no one thought I was playing with myself at the urinal. That was a sound bit of advice that I'd gotten from Taylor during one of our therapy sessions shortly after I'd gotten my packer.

"Men's bathrooms have a much different vibe from women's," he said. "You go in and do your business and get out. There isn't usually the same sort of social interaction you experience in the ladies' bathroom."

That was just fine with me. I'd always hated having to talk to anyone when I used a public bathroom anyway, and besides, if there were any risk at all of my dick falling off in front of a group of other men, I'd rather not take it.

I was feeling giddy about my new equipment and was desperate to flirt with people. I'd scroll through Facebook and check girls out from the safety of my room, but one day I saw a profile of a guy named Austin with blond, spiky hair who was friends with someone I vaguely knew from OYP. In his profile picture he had a sort of confused, awkward *What am I even doing here?* look on his face. It was so endearing—I felt like I knew that expression well—and before I could stop myself, I shot him a friend request and a message.

Hey, you're pretty cute.

He wrote back almost immediately. *Hi. Thanks.*

I figured it was best to be upfront. *I'm a trans guy.*

Several minutes passed. *Okay. That's kind of weird.*

He didn't offer anything else up, so I let it go. I couldn't afford any more insecurity in my life now that so many changes were happening.

The cruise over spring break was a total success. I passed completely. One day I was walking on the deck when I heard a girl call out, "Hey, you! You, guy!"

I slowly turned around, praying that she was calling to me. She motioned me over with her finger.

"What's up?" I said.

"There is no one else our age on this boat. We need to stick together."

That was fine by me. She was gorgeous, short with dark skin and long black hair. Her name was Hannah, and she lived in Florida. She introduced me to a few other girls she had already met, and I spent the rest of the trip hanging out with them.

I couldn't believe how much they were flirting with me, and I could openly flirt right back. That was how Wes ultimately came to terms with me as a guy—he saw that I was attracting all these hot girls. He immediately became glued to my side like we were best friends.

The only problem with the entire trip was that I couldn't take my shirt off. Whenever we went swimming or got into a hot tub, I'd have to make up some lame excuse like *I just got out of the shower and don't want to mess with my hair again* or *I got a crazy sunburn yesterday*. They'd tease me about it, but I ultimately didn't care. Even though I was stuck inside a shirt, I'd never felt freer.

13

A couple of weeks after we got back, Mom decided to let me start hormone replacement therapy. Taylor agreed that it was time, and so he wrote up his recommendation that I be put on testosterone. I then needed to take the written recommendation to a doctor. We found one who had worked with trans men patients before, and I went in for an initial round of blood work so he could figure out an appropriate dosage for me. We made another appointment for the following week, and provided that everything was normal, I'd get my first shot. I was riding high with that news and my cruise experience, and on top of all that, I was about to go to prom with a beautiful girl.

You'll recall how that went.

The following night, while catching up with Dale at OYP, it took me a few seconds to realize that the gorgeous woman who'd just walked in the door was Katie Hill. She looked so bright and *alive* compared to the time when I'd seen her at the Equality Center. I still wonder now, if I hadn't gotten dumped at prom just twenty-four hours earlier, would I have had the courage to walk right up to her?

But I did, and said, "Hi, Katie."

She turned and looked at me and smiled. "Hi, Arin," she replied.

I almost died. I couldn't believe she actually remembered my name.

I told her that I was scheduled to finally start taking testosterone later that week, and she got really excited. "Your voice is going to start cracking right after," she teased.

The music switched from Lady Gaga to that ridiculous "Cupid Shuffle" song they always play at weddings. She started dancing, and I swear she was flirting with me. She kept looking over her shoulder at me and smiling, showing off her dance moves.

I found Dale out back. "Oh my God, I want her number so bad," I said.

"Just ask," he said.

I'd never felt that nervous before. I'd started the night with such a cocky attitude, determined to make out with a girl, and here I was acting like some hand-wringing wuss.

"How do I do it?" I asked Dale. "I don't know what to do!"

He gave me a disgusted look. "Just *do it*, man."

I crossed the room with my phone in my hand. She was talking to a friend, but I interrupted and just blurted out, "Can I have your number?"

"Yeah, sure," she said. And I could tell by the tone in her

voice and by the way that she looked at me that she wasn't sure if I wanted her number because I thought she was pretty, or if I just wanted to talk about more trans stuff. She put her number into my phone and went back to talking to her friend, and I floated back to Dale, grinning and blushing.

She left not long after but gave me a hug before heading out. "Don't be a stranger—text me," she said.

Oh, I will, I thought.

When Mom came to pick me up, I couldn't shut up the entire ride home.

"Oh my God, guess who came tonight? Katie Hill! She's so pretty. I can't believe I got her number!" I babbled. "What should I do? Should I text her now? Or, like, wait a day and play it cool? I won't text her tonight. Wait. Maybe I should text her tonight so she knows I like her! No, I'll wait until morning. But late morning, so it doesn't seem like I'm desperate."

Mom just laughed at me. I could tell she was happy to see me so happy, especially after the previous night's disaster. We'd come a long way from the days when she would do anything to keep me away from a girl.

When I got home, I was shocked to see that Katie had already sent me a Facebook friend request, along with a short message saying that she hoped I'd had fun that night. I resisted the urge to write her back immediately.

I finally texted her at 10:20 the next morning:

Hey Katie, it's Arin :)

The next hour and thirty-one minutes were agonizing. But finally:

Hey Arin! What's up hun?

Just planning my day out, I think I'm going to the movies. How about you?

Pretty much the same. Did you have fun last night?

Yessss. Thank you for talking to me last night, I felt like the luck-iest guy there, getting to talk to the most beautiful girl in the room.

Stop it, you're making me blush!

I'm gonna be honest here. I'm interested in you. But if you'd just like to be friends I'm cool either way.

I held my breath while I watched those three dots appear on my iPhone, signaling that she was writing back.

Well, I admit I think you're adorable. But I just got out of a bad relationship. So we'll see. I like to get to know anyone I'm interested in anyways :) Plus I need to see if I'm right about T making your voice crack!

We continued to text flirty things throughout the day. I wanted to invite her to the movie with Mom and Wes, but I didn't have the courage after she'd told me she'd just gotten out of a bad relationship. So I was psyched when she asked if she could tag along. Of course I said yes.

She arrived at the theater a little late, wearing the same clothes as the night before, since she'd spent the night at her friend's place. I had already staked out seats far away from Mom and Wes, and she squeezed in to my left. The movie, *The Cabin in the Woods*, was just starting, so we didn't really get a chance to talk. I was fiddling with a bottle cap, and my hands were dripping sweat. I kept them firmly on my knees. Our shoulders finally touched, and we sat that way for the entire movie. That small bit of physical contact was pure, torturous heaven. I wanted so badly to put my arm around her, but I didn't want her to think I just wanted to get into her pants. I wanted her to know that I respected her, and respected the fact that she had just gotten out of a bad relationship. She had explained it a little bit in her texts—the guy had been living with her family, and then he dumped her right after she had helped him put a down payment on an apartment and a car. I couldn't imagine anyone treating her like that.

I couldn't focus on the film at all, and it was over way too fast. Mom found us in the parking lot afterward, where I made the introductions. She couldn't stop staring at Katie. It got a little awkward, so Katie hugged me and left.

"I can*not* believe that she was born a boy," Mom marveled as we got into the car. "No way. She's too pretty!"

"Told you," I said as my phone buzzed in my pocket. Katie had already texted me.

I had a really good time. :)

We kept texting a bunch of silly, sweet romantic stuff throughout the week. I called her beautiful again, and she wrote:

That's it. I'm making out with you.

She had a ton going on in her life. Besides still getting over her last boyfriend, she was wrapping up her senior year of high school while working part time. Plus, she'd found out that a mystery donor had offered to pay for her gender reassignment surgery, which was scheduled for just after her upcoming eighteenth birthday. I felt a twinge of jealousy about that, but swallowed it quickly. She was also being awarded the Carolyn Wagner Youth Leadership Award at the 2012 Equality Gala, a huge annual black-tie affair to help raise money for the Equality Center, hosted at the downtown convention center. It was a pretty big deal.

But we still found time to hang out. We met up at group at the Equality Center the Wednesday after the movie. I mostly talked about how excited I was to start taking testosterone, and she talked about how honored she was about the upcoming gala. I took her out for pizza afterward, where we chatted about places we had traveled and all the places we still wanted to go. When we were done, Katie drove me to my mom's office. We got out of the car, and Katie hugged me good-bye and then stepped back slightly, with this look in her eye that said, *So, are you gonna kiss me, or just leave me standing here?*

I had totally been planning to do it all night, but I lost my nerve at the last second. She was just too pretty. It actually made me feel sick inside, like I had no business even being near someone like her. She had these pillowy lips that absolutely paralyzed me. I'd never felt anything like that before. I was so absorbed by any little thing that came out of her mouth, and the thought of being that close to her sent little ripples of terror through my stomach and legs. *Just do it,* I was screaming in my head. But my body simply wouldn't move.

I could sense her disappointment at my lack of nerve. But I wanted our first kiss to be special, and the parking lot of Danco, with its wan fluorescent lighting and the abandoned car wash just across the street, was hardly the place to do it.

I had tickets to an upcoming Black Keys concert and asked her if she wanted to come, not realizing it was the same night as the gala. She'd already invited another friend as her guest, but she told me I should get tickets to the event.

"You could come back to my place afterward," she said. "My mom won't mind. We could put on some movies, and then Sunday my little brother has motocross practice we could watch."

Done.

On April 26, 2012, at 2:40 p.m., two days before the gala, I got my first testosterone injection. I consider it my second birthday.

The doctor came into the examining room, shuffling through the results of my blood work. I held my breath, praying that nothing was wrong.

"Well," he said. "Turns out you didn't even need a letter from your therapist."

"What do you mean?" I asked.

"All women have a normal amount of testosterone in their system. You have almost none. You could have been on at least some testosterone ages ago."

I would have been upset, if I hadn't already been so excited to start. I even let slide the fact that he had just referred to me as a woman. Still, it was weird. I guess a part of me had wondered if maybe I already had *too* much testosterone in me, and that was part of what made me trans.

He administered my dosage right there in the office to teach me how to do it at home—a long needle right in my butt cheek. There was a tiny sting, and I felt a rush of strength immediately, but it was probably psychosomatic. He gave Mom a prescription for the next shot. Our insurance had covered all of my blood work, but we had to pay out of pocket for the actual testosterone. Luckily, it isn't too expensive—my dosage costs sixty dollars for a three-month supply.

The next morning I noticed a definite physical difference. I woke up smelling really sweaty, and when I peed, the scent was thick and heavy. My skin was super-oily, and I was *starving*. I ate everything I could find in the house—cereal, toast, cookies, chicken cutlets, fruit, spaghetti. Nothing filled me up.

The morning of the gala, Katie and I went out to breakfast together at IHOP before she had to start getting ready.

"So, are YOU excitEEED about . . . ," I started to ask, but I slapped my hands over my mouth, mortified at the weird goat bleat that had just erupted from me. My voice had suddenly dropped three octaves and then scrambled up another four—it sounded like a record scratching. I froze, eyes wide, with my hands still covering my mouth, but Katie laughed so hard that bits of pancake shot out of her mouth and flew across the table.

"I told you!" she crowed. "Two days, and your voice is already cracking!"

I knew this was the sort of thing that happened to cis guys all the time through puberty. Sure, it's embarrassing to have your voice crack in the middle of saying something, let alone on a date. But I was suddenly a little thrilled inside. It was all happening—just one more step to becoming the person I was meant to be. And at the same time I was falling in love with someone who could completely understand every single thing I was going through.

Happiness that intense felt foreign to me. It had been gone from my life for so many years, and now that I was experiencing it again, I was feeling it on a level so high that nothing could burst it.

I spent all afternoon getting ready for the gala. I still had only my one black suit, the same one I wore to prom. In fact, I basically wore the entire same outfit as I had worn to prom. I wanted to buy something new and special for the occasion, but I didn't have the money. Plus, there was something sort of poetic about giving the outfit a second chance—I didn't want to look at this suit hanging in my closet and have only bad memories associated with it.

Mom was out of town, so Dad came to the gala with me. It was the first time he really got a chance to see what my new life was all about. When he picked me up, I asked if we could stop at a florist so I could get Katie a flower. I didn't want to overdo it, so I picked out a single pink rose.

When we arrived at the convention center, there was a huge line to get in, and people dressed in suits and gowns swarmed around out front. The night started with pre-party cocktails and a silent art auction, and I spotted Katie across the room as soon as we got in the door. My heart dropped. She was easily the most stunning woman there. Her hair was pulled back, with a few stray tendrils that fell down to her shoulders, and she wore a black spaghetti strap dress with a plunging neckline and a simple silver band that ran underneath her breasts. A silver necklace with a small black stone pendant hung from her neck.

"Whoa, she's gorgeous," Dad said.

"I know," I moaned, then stopped and shot him a look. "Don't act so surprised. I've got good taste."

He laughed and slapped me on the back. We watched Katie flit from one group of people to the next, clearly the biggest star of the evening. She still hadn't seen me. I suddenly shoved the flower into my Dad's hand.

"Here. I can't do it," I said, breaking into a sweat. It was like asking for her phone number all over again.

He pushed the flower back into my hand.

"Come on. Yes you can," he coaxed. "She invited you!"

I took the flower back, sucked in my breath, marched across the room, and tapped her on the back.

"Hey, Katie," I said, silently begging my voice not to crack. "I got this for you."

Her whole face lit up, and she leaned in and gave me an enormous hug. She smelled like cherry blossoms, and I closed my eyes and inhaled deeply. When I felt her lips on my neck, I almost swooned. *The celebrity of the night likes me,* I thought.

"Thank you, sweetie," she said as she pulled back, still smiling. An older man tapped her on the shoulder to introduce himself.

I backed away. "You do your thing. We'll talk after," I said, and she gave me a grateful look before turning to him.

"Nice work," Dad said when I got back over to him, and

he patted me on the shoulder again. I introduced him to a few people I knew from the Equality Center, and soon everyone headed inside the ballroom area for the awards ceremony. I couldn't concentrate on what anyone up at the podium was saying. I kept my eyes on Katie's table near the stage, where she sat with her family. When they announced her name, I clapped more loudly than anyone else.

Her speech made people cry. As she talked about her childhood struggles, her family's acceptance, and her determination to spread awareness about trans youth issues, I kept hearing sniffles from the tables around me.

She was crying too by the time she finished, and the room erupted in applause. I wanted so badly to run up and hug her. I was utterly overwhelmed with my feelings for her, and I needed to get them out. Since I couldn't actually talk to her just yet, I wrote everything I was thinking in a text. I didn't have any intention of sending it. I just wanted to record every word of what I was feeling in that exact moment.

I'm watching you with your family right now, and your speech was incredible. It's such an honor to be here as your friend, and I hope that I might one day be able to call you mine. You're such a beautiful woman, and your words are so inspiring, and I'm the luckiest guy in the room tonight just to even know you.

It went on and on like that. It was basically a massive paragraph of me vomiting up emotions. I planned to edit it down later so it didn't sound so stalkerish. But purely out of habit, I hit send.

I sunk my head into my hands in total shame, but only for a moment.

Screw it, I thought. *This is how I feel, and it's better that she knows it.*

After the rest of the speeches were over, the tables were cleared away to make room for a live band and dancing. I pushed my way through the crowd and gave Katie a huge hug. She handed her award—a heavy, marble obelisk with her name etched on the base—to her mom, and we started dancing.

"Hey, by the way," I shouted over the music, "I sent you a text by mistake. Just ignore it."

"I left my phone at home," she said, shrugging. Then she reached out and grabbed my tie, pulling me close to her. We danced pressed up against each other, the way I'd always wanted to dance with a girl but had never had the chance. The smell of her perfume overtook me again and made me all woozy.

The rest of the night was a blur of people stopping by to congratulate her, but every time we were interrupted, she kept her hand on my back and rubbed it. I stood there, beaming like an idiot. At one point the band dedicated "Wonderful Tonight" to her, and the eyes of everyone in the room were on us.

As the dance wound down, we made our way outside and took some pictures. Dad walked me over to his car so I could get my overnight bag.

"Have fun, but don't have *too* much fun," he said. "Don't drink any alcohol. Be cool."

"Okay, Dad," I said, and hugged him good-bye. I ran back over to Katie's family. Her brother had borrowed a huge Hummer from a friend to chauffer her around in, and I climbed into the backseat with her.

When we got to Katie's house, a sense of déjà vu washed over me. I'd seen photos of this tan, one-story building before, in the *Tulsa World* article, and I suddenly felt like I'd been transported into a movie. The interior was small but supercozy and inviting. Katie led me into the living room just off their kitchen and proceeded to build a massive bed on the floor out of seven or eight different blankets and pillows that she leaned up against the base of the couch.

"Pick out a movie and make yourself comfortable," she said. "I'm going to go change out of this dress."

I wandered over to the stack of DVDs and selected the scariest one I could find, the fourth installment of the Final Destination franchise. I knew it would be full of gory death scenes that would give me an excuse to put my arm around her.

She came back a few minutes later. She still had her makeup on, but she'd changed into a pair of pajama bottoms and a tank top.

"Your turn," she said. "My room is just down the hall. Oh, and I got your text." It looked like she was fighting back tears. "Thank you. It means . . . a lot. I still wasn't sure if you really felt that way about me."

"You have *no* idea," I said, and left to change.

Her bedroom was tiny, with a single twin bed. The walls were painted purple and cream. I unzipped my bag and stripped, laying my suit gently down on her bed, careful not to wrinkle it. I threw on a pair of gym shorts and a T-shirt, and was in the middle of adjusting my binder when I heard her scream from down the hallway.

I ran out of her room, in the direction the sound had come from. The bathroom door was open, and she was sitting on the closed toilet, holding her foot and wincing. There was blood dripping from her big toe. Her award was lying on the floor next to her.

"I dropped it," she said, looking up at me.

I kneeled in front of her. "Let me see."

The cut itself wasn't too bad, but it was bleeding pretty heavily. Jazzlyn, Katie's mom, appeared in the doorway.

"Oh, honey, hang on. I'll get the first aid kit."

I cleaned the wound and kept pressure on it to try to stop the bleeding. Jazzlyn returned with the kit, and we took turns fussing over Katie, putting antiseptic on her toe and wrapping it up in a bandage.

Katie kept making self-deprecating comments about how she was so clumsy and such an idiot. It killed me to hear her talk about herself that way.

"Come on. Stop it," I said. "It's kind of funny. I mean, why do they make these things so heavy?" I picked the award up off the floor. It must have weighed about seven pounds. "It's not your fault—you could actually kill someone with this thing."

I helped her into the living room and was showing her the movie I had picked out, just as her mom appeared. "I made pizza rolls!" Jazzlyn announced. She set down a plate of those little frozen pepperoni things and went back into the kitchen.

I had a two-second silent debate with myself. I try to never eat processed foods, but I wasn't about to be rude. Before I could even reach for one myself, though, Katie stuck one into my mouth. I started to gag but tried not to show it. I mean, when a girl feeds you something, you eat it.

"Mmmmm," I managed to mumble halfheartedly as I tried to swallow it.

Jazzlyn came back into the room with two glasses of root beer, and set them down on the coffee table. I was desperate for something to wash the taste of the appetizer out of my mouth, and I reached a little too fast for the glass and knocked it over. The soda fizzed and hissed all over the surface, and raced to the edge of the table and dripped onto the floor. *Nice one,* I thought. I turned to Katie with a helpless look on my face, still choking on the pizza roll. Jazzlyn ran into the kitchen for some paper towels, and they couldn't stop laughing at me.

I hadn't even been there for thirty minutes, and already everything was a disaster. I kept apologizing as I followed her mom into the kitchen to wash the sticky soda off my arm and hands.

We finally got settled on the blankets, and her mom flicked off the lights and left us alone as the movie started. The opening scene is a massive orgy of death as teenagers are impaled and crushed left and right during a NASCAR-style speedway race accident. People get sliced in half, crushed by flying motors, burned up in flames. It was perfect. We had started out leaning against the sofa but slid down onto the blankets as the screams on the TV got louder. I gathered up all my courage. *Screw it. I'm going for it,* I thought as I slid my arm around her back. I braced myself for her reaction.

I didn't need to worry. She immediately turned and curled her entire body against me, throwing one leg over my stomach and resting a hand on my chest, over my binder. All the tension that had been building between us eased up but was suddenly replaced by a whole new fear: *How far can I take this?*

I knew she could probably feel the edge of my binder underneath my shirt, and I worried for a second that it would be a turnoff. But then I felt her bulge against my leg and knew I had nothing to worry about. We were both dealing with equipment issues, and her issue canceled out any concern I had about mine. We knew who we were—a boy and a girl, cuddling together, watching a scary movie. Even through all the fear and anticipation of what might come next, it was the most normal I'd ever felt in my life.

She suddenly sat up a little and looked down at me. I stared up at her. She moved her face really close to mine, like an inch away, and held it there for about thirty seconds, but it felt like forever. I could feel her breath on my lips, and I knew she had to feel my heart pounding in my chest. It was so intimate, and I didn't want the moment to end. The screams of the dying people on the television faded away, and she broke that last distance between us and kissed me.

It wasn't a heavy kiss; it was very soft and sweet. Small, gentle kisses at first, for probably ten full minutes. And then it was on. At some point I paused and asked, "Will you be my girlfriend?"

She kissed me again and said yes.

I kept my underwear and binder on all night like I always had with Darian, even though I felt so much safer about my body with Katie. I didn't have to feel self-conscious about my need for those barriers, because she understood why I had them. Hours after our first kiss, I looked up and saw the sky turning blue out the window. I held her tight, and we finally passed out. We got only about two hours of sleep before it was time to get up and go to her brother's motocross practice. We each ran to the bathroom to wipe ourselves down with a washcloth, and then jumped into the car with her mom and brother. We made out in the backseat the whole way there while they politely pretended not to notice. Now that the physical barrier had been broken between us, we couldn't keep our hands off each other.

Once we got to the track, we just kept making out. No one around us batted an eye—we were just two horny straight kids going at it.

After the race was over, we went back to her house and collapsed into a hammock in her backyard, talking and kissing. I'd never taken any drugs but figured that must have been what it felt like to be high on ecstasy or something. It was pure euphoria, and she told me she felt the same way.

She slipped her hand under my shirt, and then under my binder. "You're, what, a B cup?" she asked.

"Don't remind me," I said, squirming away and pulling her hand out. All of the old shame and embarrassment about my body came creeping back for a moment.

"That's just the size I want. Wouldn't it be perfect if we could just swap everything?"

"I'd do anything to have your dick," I said, totally serious. "It's the perfect size."

"You can have it," she said.

From that day forward we were together every chance we got. Mom seemed to really like Katie, and let her stay over at our house a lot.

"Did you get rid of all your girl clothes?" Katie asked me one day.

"I put them all in garbage bags. I think Mom took them to the Goodwill."

But it turned out she hadn't yet—the bags were still in our attic. We dragged them downstairs, and Katie went to town. It turned out that we have the same waist size, and since we're almost the same height, everything fit her perfectly.

"I can really have this?" she kept asking. "And this?"

"Take it all," I said as she sorted out a huge pile of blouses, jeans, and skirts, many of them with the tags still on. I was engrossed with a mirror, obsessively running my hands over the bumps on my Adam's apple. It was getting huge, but even better—the time when I usually got my period had come and gone. I was blood-stain-free and still reveling in clearing that hurdle.

Later that day Katie and I were messing around down behind my house, barefoot in the mud on the banks of the little stream that runs through the valley.

"So," she asked slowly, "are you going to let me list you as my boyfriend on Facebook?"

"I was just gonna ask you the same thing!" I said. I'd wanted to make us "Facebook official" since our first night together but was still a little nervous about coming on too strong and too fast in our relationship. She'd told me more about her ex, Hawthorne. They had broken up only a couple of weeks back, and the last thing I wanted was to be her rebound.

It turned out, I didn't have to worry. One afternoon I was on top of her on my bed, staring down at her, and I couldn't keep it inside any longer.

"I have something I want to say," I said.

She smiled like she knew what was coming. "Yeah?"

"I love you."

There was a long pause, and I was terrified that she wouldn't say it back, but she did. We held each other and laughed, rolling around on top of the covers. Nothing, not even sex, feels as good as getting a first "I love you" out into the open, and then having it tossed back at you to catch.

I'd never felt love this pure or strong before, though. It was nothing like the emotions I'd experienced while longing for Darian, because Katie was actually there—I could touch her, hug her, and kiss her. I could take her to all my favorite spots in the woods, and she understood everything about how nature itself made me feel more spiritual than church ever could. While I'd been hesitant to tell my OYP friends that I'd grown up Christian, I could tell Katie everything about my changing idea of God. For a long time after getting kicked out of Lincoln, I'd turned my back on any idea of him. Or her. Or whatever. But as I became happier with myself, I began to slowly get back in touch with that side of myself. And Katie understood. She took the same broad view toward religion that I now accepted—that as long as you cared for other people and took actions to help them, you were respecting whatever idea it was you had of God.

We were completely in sync with our worldviews, and because of that, things kept getting more and more intense between us physically. I still kept my underwear and binder on when we made out, but we felt ourselves needing to get closer. Even though our genders didn't match our bodies, we each still had working parts that *wanted* to fit together. And since she was getting her surgery soon, we knew that wouldn't always be the case.

One night when we were making out, she asked if I had a condom.

"No," I said. "I never really had any reason to get them."

"See what you can do," she said. She looked down between her legs. "This thing is going to be gone soon. And I've never had hetero sex before. Have you?"

I shook my head. "I'm a virgin in that regard," I said.

"I want to do this with you while I still can. It's going to be our only opportunity. What do you think?"

As uncomfortable as I was with my vagina, I wanted to as well. I'm a man stuck in a female body, but the parts I was born with still have the ability to feel good. And since Katie had the same dysphoria about her own genitals, I felt safer about making myself that vulnerable.

At school the next day I approached a group of kids I still hung out with sometimes, and targeted one of them named John, who was always bragging about his sexual escapades.

"Dude, um, do you think you can get me a condom?"

"What size?" he asked without skipping a beat.

"I don't know, regular?" I said. It wasn't like I had anything to compare hers to.

"No problem," he said. He knew I was trans but was cool enough to not ask me any detailed questions about why I needed one. A few hours later I passed him in the hallway, and he slipped a square piece of clear plastic into my hand. I cupped my palm and glanced down at it, making sure no one could see.

"Why is it *green*?" I whispered.

He shrugged. "Beats me. Have fun!"

When Katie came over that following Friday night, I dimmed the lights in my room and put Band of Horses on my stereo. Moonlight streamed through the windows.

"Did you get one?" she asked, stretching out on the bed.

"Yup," I said, digging the cucumber-colored prophylactic out of my wallet. I cringe now when I think of my sexual etiquette, but I was so terrified that I just tossed it at her, and it landed on her stomach. "There you go," I said.

She put it aside and reached out to me. And as soon as we started making out, all of my fear disappeared.

I kept my shirt and binder on, but when we finally made love, it didn't occur to me for even one second that my girlfriend was putting her penis inside me. I was still a man, and she was still a woman, and this was simply a way for us to be as physically close to each other as humanly possible.

14

Katie graduated from high school the day before her eighteenth birthday, and the day after that she was set to leave for San Francisco to get her surgery. I was still secretly jealous that a donor was paying for it all, but I continued to bury that thought whenever it bubbled to the surface. I knew that she deserved the gift. She had been working so hard for trans awareness in the Tulsa area for more than a year, giving speeches and interviews, and there was no way her family could have afforded to pay for the procedures themselves. The same donor was also paying for her college tuition at University of Tulsa, provided she kept up at least a 3.0 GPA. Which I knew wouldn't be a problem for her.

"Forget 3.0. I'm going to get straight As," she told me. I didn't doubt it. She could talk about any subject—politics, religion, the economy, art—with an air of authority that bordered on intimidating. My entire family, including Papa and Gigi, fell in love with her almost as much as I did.

I went to the mall the day before her graduation to shop

for something to wear. I bought a shirt and a blue tie, and stopped by Spalon for a quick trim. I wanted to look perfect for her.

Mom came with me to Katie's ceremony. As the school principal was calling out all the students' names in alphabetical order, I turned to my mom and said, "Isn't this incredible?"

"That she's graduating? Sure."

"No," I said. "Do you realize that it was exactly one year ago today that I first read the article about Katie? And now she's my *girlfriend*."

"Yeah, that is pretty crazy," she mused.

"You and I have come a long way, and I just want you to know how much I appreciate all your support."

She squeezed my hand as the name "Katie Hill" came booming out of the speakers, and we leapt to our feet and cheered.

Our families went to dinner together at a Mexican restaurant called Los Cabos that night. Katie had changed into a black skirt and a red blousy top, and I sat next to her at the head of the table. I tried to concentrate on the conversation, but all I could think about was that after one more day, she was going to leave for two weeks. What if something went wrong? I couldn't be by her side for what would probably be the most important moment of her entire life.

And in addition to that concern, the jealousy I kept trying to suppress continued to push to the surface of my brain. I couldn't help it. I knew that I'd be getting top surgery at some point, but she was getting a vagina, and I'd still be stuck with mine.

In a way, though, I did already have a new, *very* small penis. One of the other big side effects of being on testosterone is that it causes the clitoris to grow larger and longer. Mine was the size of a Tic Tac after just two days on T, and by Katie's graduation, it was a respectable little member and was still growing every day. But it wasn't anything I could pee out of or use for penetration.

Sex reassignment surgery for a male-to-female vagina (usually called "bottom surgery") has gotten pretty advanced. The most commonly used procedure—the one Katie was getting—is called a vaginoplasty, and in the most basic of explanations, the testicles are removed and the shaft of the penis is inverted to create a vaginal canal. A clit is formed using the more sensitive skin from the head of the penis. The new vagina needs to remain open, and this is often accomplished with something called a dilator (basically a medical-grade dildo), so the body doesn't treat the vaginal opening as a wound and try to close it up. Dilation needs to be done several times a day in the weeks after the surgery, and then once or twice a week for the rest of the person's life. But once healed, the result is usually indistinguishable from any other vagina.

Female-to-male bottom surgery, however, is a lot more complicated. Right now there are two types—metoidioplasty and phalloplasty. Again, I'm just going to provide the most basic of descriptions. If you want really detailed reports, you can find tons of information online.

Metoidioplasty is an umbrella term for several different surgeries, and you can choose to do any number of them, or just one. Essentially, though, a surgeon creates a small penis out of a clit that's been enlarged by testosterone.

The first and main step is a clitoral release. The tissue underneath the clit is removed, which lifts it up and out, exposing more length. The doctor can then perform a circumcision on the skin around the clit if you like. You can stop there, or continue with additional surgeries like urethroplasty, where the doctor will reroute the urethra through the clit so you can pee out of it standing up. You can also get scrotoplasty, where skin from the outer labia is used to create ball sacs with silicone testicles; a vaginectomy, which removes the vagina; and a hysterectomy, which is surgery to remove the uterus.

The cool thing about metoidioplasty is all of the different choices available—you can mix and match to come up with what's right for you. The downside is that your junk isn't going to be that big. But for me, and a lot of other trans men, that's hardly a deal breaker. I'd personally rather look in the mirror and see a man with a small penis looking back at me than see a man with a vagina.

If size is really important to someone, they can opt for phalloplasty, but it is a much, much more involved form of surgery, not to mention crazy expensive. While metoidioplasty can run anywhere from roughly $2,000 to $40,000, depending on the doctor and how many of the options you go for, phalloplasty tends to start at around $50,000 and can go as high as $150,000. It involves lengthening the urethra and building a penis out of skin taken from a donor site somewhere on the body. (Once again, this is a *totally* simplistic description.) It's a major operation, and there are a lot more ways that things could go wrong. But on the upside, you can pick the penis size.

I was leaning toward metoidioplasty because you can go in stages, and it doesn't hinder the ability to get a phalloplasty in the future. But the key word was "future." At that point bottom surgery was still low on my list of transitioning importance. I wanted to see how testosterone would continue to change my body (I'd started growing hair on my ass—a new development that I wasn't exactly thrilled about), and get top surgery first. And I also wanted to be 100 percent positive about which bottom surgery option was right for me.

And truth be told, at that exact moment I was more concerned about what Katie's impending surgery meant for the future of our relationship. Would she still even want to be with me when she got back? Or would she want to be with a guy who had a fully functioning penis? I shifted my legs nervously and felt the comforting weight of my packer, but it didn't do much to suppress my anxiety. Maybe I'd need to move bottom surgery higher up on my list.

I watched Katie's profile as she laughed with her brother, and did my best to push the thoughts out of my head. This was *her* night, *her* weekend, and I wasn't going to spoil it with my moping. Our love was so much stronger than what was between our legs.

We celebrated her birthday at OYP the next night. The place was packed with people, including her friend Michael, who had been her official guest at the gala. I knew that he had feelings for her, but she had always made it clear to him that they would only ever be friends, so I didn't feel threatened. In fact, I liked him.

The three of us were standing against a wall, taking a break from dancing, when suddenly Katie got a weird look on her face.

"Oh no," she said.

I followed her gaze toward the door. A tall blond guy had just walked in and was scanning the room.

"Who's that?" I asked.

"It's her ex, Hawthorne," Michael said.

I immediately tensed up and narrowed my eyes at him. I felt my shoulders rise up and back, almost like how an animal will attempt to make itself look bigger when cornered.

Katie turned to me. "I'd better go talk to him," she said.

"Do you want me to come with you?" I asked.

She shook her head. "It would probably make things worse. Don't worry, I've got this under control."

Michael and I kept a close watch on her as she made her way through the crowd and pulled Hawthorne off to the side.

"I'm going to beat the crap out of him if he hurts her," I told Michael, surprising myself. It had to be the testosterone speaking—I'd never said anything like that in my life. But I meant it.

"I'm with you," Michael said. "That guy is an asshole. I bet you anything he's trying to get back together with her."

We watched Hawthorne storm out the door, and Katie came back over to us. Michael had been right.

"I told him I have someone else in my life who would

never treat me like he did," Katie said, and kissed me on the cheek.

The song that was playing ended, and one of the volunteers got on the microphone. "Katie Hill, where are you? Get on up here!"

She blushed and made her way to the stage, where the guy grabbed her hand and lifted it up. "Today is Katie's birthday, and she's leaving tomorrow to get her gender reassignment surgery!"

Everyone in the room cheered and clapped and sang "Happy Birthday." I saw her wipe a tear from her eye.

We danced some more and left not long after. We stopped at a gas station and picked up a six-pack of cream soda and took it back to her house, where I gave her the birthday gift I'd picked out, a silver charm bracelet with two charms on it—a butterfly, to represent her transformation, and a heart.

"That one's because I love you," I said. "Oh, and I brought this, too."

I jumped off her bed and reached for my bag, and handed her one of my old cross-country shirts that she'd always liked.

"You can wear it in California," I said.

"Thank you," she said, "for both." She held the shirt up to her face. "It smells like you."

She went to her dresser and opened a drawer. "You need something of mine to wear," she said. She pulled out her favorite hoodie, a black one with thumbholes and a few gray swirly designs on the sleeves.

"It will be like we're holding each other when we put them on," she said.

We crawled under a blanket on her bed and stared at the clock, too excited to sleep, like kids on Christmas Eve.

"Are you scared?" I asked.

"No," she said. "Not at all. I've been waiting for this my entire life."

"I know what you mean. Are you *sure* they can't just give me your penis?"

She smiled, but by then it had already become an old joke.

I almost started crying at the airport the next morning, but managed to hold it together as we said good-bye. She was so giddy, and I didn't want anything to distract her from that feeling.

"I'll call when I land," she promised, and then she was gone.

As Jazzlyn followed her toward the security line, she turned and looked back at me. "Now, don't go getting a new girlfriend while she's gone," she said. "Don't forget about Katie!"

"Um, that's pretty much impossible," I answered.

Six hours later I got a video message from Katie. She was standing in front of a palm tree, and the sky behind it was a gorgeous pale blue. She had my long-sleeved shirt on.

"It's hot as hell here," she said. "But I'm wearing this anyway. Love you!"

We talked, texted, and used FaceTime constantly during the days leading up to the actual surgery.

"See you on the other side," I said in our last conversation. "I love you. Everything is going to be okay."

Mom let me stay home from school that day. I paced relentlessly through Danco, until she finally told me to go outside. I walked over to a nearby lot with an empty office building on it and sat down on the curb, tapping my foot and checking my phone for the millionth time. Suddenly Dad appeared next to me.

"You've got to relax," he said, just as a strange rustling sound began off to our left. We turned and saw pages of grimy newspaper swirling up off the ground in a perfect funnel. They twirled higher and higher, taking on the shape of a six-foot-tall tornado. I'd seen plenty of small wind swirls on the ground in my life, but never anything as big as this one.

The papers suddenly shot straight up into the air and disappeared over the side of the building.

"That was weird," Dad said, cocking his head to one side.

I didn't say it out loud, but it felt like a sign. Like all of Katie's pain was vanishing. Like it was actually possible for all of the tormented parts of our lives to be swept away, leaving us with a clean slate to start again.

I got a text from Jazzlyn late in the afternoon, with a photo of Katie sleeping. *She did great,* it said.

I didn't hear from Katie herself until I was in history class the next morning.

Hey, baby. I'm out. How are you?

I hid my phone under the desk as I typed back.

How am I doing? How are YOU doing? You just got your penis turned inside out!

I waited for a response, and a few minutes later a picture

of something black and red and blue popped up, followed by a smiley face. It took me a few seconds to realize what I was looking at.

So proud of you, baby, I wrote. *But you might want to wait and heal a little before sending me any sexy pics.*

For those first few days she was pretty drugged up and loopy, and I amassed an arsenal of blackmail-worthy videos and texts from her while she was on morphine. But even though she was always either high or in pain, her happiness radiated through the mental haze.

Right after Katie returned, we went to Papa and Gigi's lake house for the weekend. I was worried that she needed to relax in bed, but she insisted it was better for her to be up and moving around. She wore her only bathing suit—a black bikini with a skirt bottom that previously hid her bulge.

"I guess we'd better go shopping for some new swim-wear," I said. She was perched on the prow of Papa's speed-boat like a figurehead, and the lake glistened all around her, reflecting off her skin.

My binder suddenly felt extra tight and sweaty under my T-shirt. I pictured myself stripping it off, my chest some-how magically flat, and joining her up at the top of the boat. I imagined what the sun would feel like on my bare skin, and suddenly little licks of the lake breeze found their way inside my shirt, only to be stopped short by the extra fabric. It was a cruel tease, but seeing how peaceful Katie looked less-ened my jealousy over her newfound freedom. I was happy because she was happy.

We stayed up all night, kissing and laughing. Since she would still be healing for up to three months, we were limited in how far we could go. But it didn't matter to me at all at first. It was the best summer of my life. We went on long camping trips out at the lake with Dale and other friends from OYP, and failed miserably at trying to scale the fish we'd catch. We went on a Color Run, a five-K race where at five different checkpoints organizers would blow huge clouds of brightly hued dust all over us. The sweat made it stick to our bodies, and by the end we were two rainbow-covered messes. I blew pixie snot out of my nose for a week.

We had so much fun at the race that Katie decided we should throw our own sort of flying-dust party. So one afternoon when Dale's parents were out of town, Katie and I met him and his girlfriend at his house with several twenty-five-pound bags of flour. We all chased one another through a homemade sprinkler we'd made by duct-taping onto his hose a two-liter soda bottle with a bunch of holes punched into it, and we tossed handfuls of white powder at one another. Soon we were a goopy mess and collapsed on the ground, cracking up under the sun. But suddenly I felt my skin start to stiffen. I looked around and noticed that Dale and Katie were clawing at their arms and legs.

"What is going on?" I yelled. "I feel like I'm turning to stone!"

That was when it hit me. Flour and water are what papier-mâché is made out of! We spent the rest of the afternoon trying to get the gluey, rapidly hardening second skin off us.

Despite all the fun, I was worried about Dale. He still wasn't out to his family, because they were so homophobic. They called him Tanya, and it was really starting to mess with his head.

"I keep trying to get the courage up," he told us as we scraped and wiped the goo from our bodies. "I get it all planned out in my head, but then I chicken out. I'm pretty sure they'd kick me to the curb."

"Then you can just come live with me," I decided. "I bet my mom would be cool with it."

He smiled faintly. "Thanks. But it's not the same. I wish my family were like both of yours."

Katie and I glanced at each other, feeling helpless.

"We're always here for you," was all I could think to say.

A few weeks later, *Tulsa World* did a follow-up story on Katie's life postsurgery, and my name appeared in the paper as her new boyfriend. It made me feel that much more official when we marched in the Tulsa gay pride parade together the following weekend with a bunch of other kids from OYP. Katie and I dressed in corresponding handmade FTM (female-to-male) and MTF (male-to-female) T-shirts, and held hands the entire way. I took her swing dancing, and she wore a simple black dress that I had worn to a formal dinner on the cruise where I'd first bonded with Darian. It looked a million times better on Katie than it ever had on me. She knew how to walk in it, how to make it hug and curve around her body when she moved. When I first saw her in it, I had a small flash of unease, remembering how constricting it had felt on me, how I'd torn it off and thrown it into a corner as soon as the dinner had ended. It was like a ghost coming back to haunt me.

But seeing her inside a part of my past was also oddly comforting, as if she'd been with me this whole time and I just hadn't realized it.

One night we were camping with Dale and a few other friends. They busted out guitars, and I grabbed a small bongo drum, and we all started playing music and singing songs. Some we knew, some we made up, and I was lost in a little reverie, when I noticed that Katie had withdrawn from the group and was sitting with her knees up to her chest, far back from the fire. I stopped playing and got up to sit beside her.

"What's up?" I asked.

"You're all so talented," she said quietly.

"What are you talking about? We're just screwing around. I'm sure we'd sound awful to anyone who walked by."

"I don't have any talents," she said, staring into the fire.

"Are you kidding? You're probably the most gifted person I know!" I couldn't figure out where this was coming from; I'd never seen her doubt herself before.

"You know that things are going to get really intense for me when school starts, right?" she asked.

"Yeah, of course," I said.

"I just mean, I'm not going to have as much time to hang out. I have to study really hard to keep my grades up. And I'm going to be making new friends."

"Wait, what are you saying?" I asked, getting nervous.

"Nothing, really. I just want to make sure we both have the same realistic expectations. You're starting your junior year of high school, but college is a whole different world."

"But I'll still get to see you. We're going to stay together, right?" I was starting to panic.

"Yes, of course," she said. "I just want you to be prepared for this to change. It might be a shock, since we see each other every day right now."

I relaxed. "I can handle that," I said. "You know I support you no matter what."

OYP held their annual summer prom, and I was determined to give the tradition another shot. My disastrous night with Jessica felt like it had happened in another lifetime, but in reality it had been only a couple of months before. I decided to go with a more casual look instead of a full suit, so I put on slacks and a vest over a white button-down shirt and a tie. I was especially excited because I'd started getting the first few hairs on my chin. I couldn't stop touching them, and would even massage my face to try to make more grow in.

Katie wore the same beautiful dress she'd worn to the gala. The prom theme was "Masquerade," and everything was decorated in purple and green. I saw Dale and gave him a hug.

"Vote for me for prom king!" he said.

"I'll vote for you if you vote for me," I said, half-joking.

"Done!"

We danced our asses off, took tons of photos, played with the balloons that were flying everywhere, caught up with friends—all the normal, dumb, innocent things that are supposed to happen at prom. But it *mattered*. Everyone who was there had been robbed of this experience in some way or another, by not being able to be themselves at their own school's prom.

Toward the end of the night the DJ stopped the music and announced it was time to name the prom king and queen.

"Our finalists for king, Arin Andrews and Dale Martin!"

We looked at each other, shrugged, and ran onto the stage together. The DJ made the final decision based on how loud the crowd cheered for each us, and I was convinced that Dale had won, until I heard my name and felt a crown placed on my head. I barely had time to register what had happened before the DJ shoved us aside.

"And now for your queen!"

He rattled off about nine names, including Katie's. As the girls filed onto the stage, I realized that all of her competitors were drag queens, vamped up to the extreme with glitter and giant wigs and heavy makeup. They preened and posed while Katie stood in the center, smiling nervously.

She won the cheer vote by a landslide. As she was being crowned, I saw one of the drag queens, clearly disappointed by the loss, turn to Katie and say, "Who the hell are *you*?" before stomping offstage.

The lights dimmed and the floor cleared as the DJ ushered us down for our dance. He played "True Colors" by Cyndi Lauper, and for the first half of the song it was just the two of us out there, holding on to each other. We kissed, and when I heard the crowd scream wildly, I realized half of them hadn't even known we were a couple to begin with. I felt like I was living the happy ending of a 1980s teen movie, right down to the song.

But real life keeps going after the credits roll. And the happy ending is just there to please an audience. And, boy, were we about to get an audience.

15

One day in August I got a call from Katie. "So, something awesome just happened," she said. "A media company found me on Facebook, and they want to come out and film us talking about our relationship. Apparently they saw that follow-up piece that *Tulsa World* did on me, the one that mentioned you. I gave them your number so they could talk to you about it."

"What do they want to film?" I asked. "Is it like a news show?"

"No, I don't think so exactly," she said. "They want to do a video on us that's just about how we're a trans teen couple in love. They'll run it in England and then also try to get us news coverage here, too."

It sounded a little confusing, but I said okay. I'd seen how much good Katie had done for our local trans community in terms of raising awareness, and I loved the idea of being able to help out too in any way I could. I got a call shortly thereafter from the producer, who kept assuring me that they weren't out to exploit us.

I told him he'd have to talk to Mom, so I gave him her number. I probably would have forgotten about the whole thing, except suddenly plans were being made, and the next thing I knew, a camera crew showed up at our front door.

Everyone was perfectly nice. The producers interviewed Katie and me together and then one-on-one. We talked about our life stories up until that point, and explained how we'd met and fallen in love. They did a regular still photo shoot too, and it was fun, I guess, but Katie *really* enjoyed it. She loved having her hair and face done, and I couldn't blame her. She was great with lipstick and mascara, but having professional makeup artists working on her took it to a whole other level. She looked like a model. And she was a natural in front of the camera. She always knew exactly what to say—somehow understanding like an expert the right time to make a joke versus the right time to be serious.

I felt way more awkward. I think maybe it was because she had already had her surgery, which then put me in the position of having to explain that I hadn't had anything done yet. I was quick to let them know that it was part of my plan, though.

They finally wrapped up and went home. Life continued as normal for a week or two, until the first story about us appeared in a British paper. We clicked on the website link, and I sat back in shock. There was a photo of us, and the caption was something like: *Meet the Transgender Teen Couple: "We're in Love and We Want Babies!"*

"I never said that!" I was horrified.

Katie laughed it off. "Look, any exposure for the community is good."

A couple of days later we got a call from the producers of the original story, saying that *Inside Edition* wanted to do a story on us. That was when things really took off. A bigger film crew came out to my house, and we went through all the motions again, telling the same story of how we'd met, how she could wear my old clothes, how great it would be if we could just swap genitals.

This time the answers and stories rolled easily off my tongue, like an encore performance. We knew what they wanted to hear and had perfected the lines.

While I was cool with talking about my experiences transitioning so far, a part of me still craved the stealth anonymity that the cruise had afforded me—a world where no one had ever known me as Emerald. So I switched schools again, to a much larger place called Owasso that's known to have better academics than Catoosa. It honestly didn't occur to me that anyone in my town would actually see the television interview Katie and I had just recorded. There was still this sort of unreality about seeing myself on television, like I was a character. School was my real life. And amidst the more than three thousand students that attended Owasso, I figured I could fly under the radar.

Mom came with me on the first day to talk to the school counselor. The sheer amount of students milling about was totally daunting. I couldn't imagine talking to anyone, but as we made our way down the hallway, I saw a girl with cropped hair wearing a big rainbow bracelet. As we passed by her, I turned to Mom and said loudly, "Gee, I wonder if they have any sort of LGBT student alliance here."

The girl whipped her head around. "We do!" she called out.

I smiled and waved. Even though I had no intention of joining—I still wanted to lie low—it was comforting just to know that there was one if I ever wanted to get involved.

The school secretary ushered us into a counselor's office for my new-student orientation. "Let's see," the counselor said, shuffling around some papers on her desk. "Oops, I think they gave me the wrong file." She started to stand up.

"No, they didn't," Mom said, all business. "Emerald goes by 'Arin' and uses the male pronoun. He's transgender."

I didn't even have time to brace myself for a reaction, before the counselor smiled. "Not a problem at all," she said. "I'll inform all of the teachers."

She went on to tell me that I could use the bathroom in the nurse's office, and that according to my transcripts, I'd already fulfilled all of Owasso's gym requirements back at Lincoln, so locker rooms wouldn't be an issue. The school was totally accommodating.

I completely passed as male among the student body, but I had a hard time focusing on anything the first week. All I could think about was Katie starting her new college life. And it didn't help that I didn't hear from her at all.

Her classes had started a week earlier, and Jazzlyn and I had helped her move all of her stuff into her dorm room. It looked like a cinder block cage, and the entire building smelled like some sort of strong disinfectant trying to cover up the scent of dirty diapers. But at least she had a single instead of having to deal with a roommate.

As I helped her hang up her clothes, I realized that half of them used to be mine. *At least they'll get an education,* I thought.

Before my mom came to pick me up, I wrote Katie a note telling her how much I loved her, and slipped it inside one of her textbooks so she'd find it later. Katie came downstairs and hugged me good-bye, but I felt really uneasy as my mom and I pulled away from campus. All around us were hundreds of teenagers unpacking their cars, and in my mind they all had the same look in their eyes—*Time to get laid.*

I knew I had to give Katie space so that she could get established, but after spending almost every single day with her since we'd first met, the sudden silence between us was jarring. I kept in the front of my mind our conversation by the fire over the summer—she was going to need time to focus on her work. But when she canceled our plans to meet up on the weekend after my first week at school, we got into our first real fight.

It happened over the phone. "We went over this. I'm going to need time to settle in," she said, sounding annoyed. "This is a huge deal for me, and I've got to start out right. I can't lose my benefactor."

"I know all that, and I totally understand, but we also agreed that we'd make time for each other."

"I know you think you understand, but I don't think you can."

There was a distance in her voice that freaked me out. She finally agreed to come over one night during the following week. And when we saw each other in person, everything was fine. We built a fire outside and cuddled by the flames, letting the smoke blow over us so the warm, woodsy scent would permeate our clothing.

"The classes are way harder than I thought," she said. "It's a lot to keep up with. What about yours?"

"Tougher than Catoosa but easier than Lincoln," I said. "And everyone knows me as a guy. I don't think anyone suspects. All the teachers are so cool—there hasn't been a single pronoun slipup."

"See?" she said. "Everything is working out for us. And even though I can't see you as much, I'm not going anywhere," she reassured me.

I really wanted to believe her, but the fact was, we rarely had sex anymore. There was only so much we could do over the summer while she healed, and now that she *had* healed, we hardly saw each other. It was almost starting to feel like Darian all over again—a relationship in words only.

I figured if Katie was studying extra hard, then I should too. I threw myself into my schoolwork and stayed under the radar at school, not attempting to make any new friends. Katie kept her promise and made more time for me on the weekends. I took her swing dancing a few more times with my CAP friends, but I never really met any of her college friends. That part of her life remained separate.

The one and only time I met some of the new people in her life, she invited me to play paintball on campus. She picked me up at my house and introduced me to the two guys in her car, Mark and Justin.

"What's up?" I said. They mumbled hello.

Katie had to sneak me onto the campus, since only students were allowed to participate in the game. I was nervous, but she reassured me.

"Don't worry," she said. "You look old enough. Look at all your facial hair!"

I was happy she'd noticed that even more had grown in recently, but then I heard one of the guys mutter from the backseat: "You've got the kind of face that I hate."

"What?" I asked, turning around.

"Nothing," Justin said, refusing to meet my eye.

I looked at Katie, but she just stared straight ahead, pretending to concentrate on the road. We were silent for the rest of the ride, but as soon as we parked and the two guys walked a few feet ahead of us, I pounced.

"What the hell was that all about?" I asked.

"What?" she asked.

"That remark about my face. Why didn't you stick up for me?"

"Oh, that's just his personality," she said. "Ignore it. Besides, you could have stuck up for yourself."

The rest of the day got worse from there. I felt uncomfortable around all the older college kids, who ignored me. I played a pretty lackluster game of paintball, and Katie drove me home after. She never asked me back to campus.

I mentioned to my friend Jon from CAP that I wasn't getting to spend as much time with Katie, and he offered to take both of us flying. I was psyched, but when Katie arrived at Jones Riverside, a small-craft airport that offers rentals to anyone with a pilot's license, she was in a foul mood and barely spoke.

We climbed into a white Cessna 172 with red stripes on the nose and tail. I sat in the backseat with Katie, and we took off down the runway. I held her hand and kept trying to make eye contact to smile at her, but she just stared out the window, so I gave up and did the same. The Arkansas River glistened and snaked below us as we reached five thousand feet, and Jon banked sharply and headed toward downtown Tulsa. We did a quick cruise by the Bank of Oklahoma Center before heading back out toward the open countryside.

The sun was starting to inch down closer to the horizon line as we landed, and the plane's wingtips lit up with orange and red streaks, like feathers on a phoenix. When we all got out, Katie thanked Jon, gave me a perfunctory hug, and left.

"See?" I said as she walked away.

"Yeah, she's acting weird," he said. "But college is tough. Give her some more time to get settled."

It had been almost two months. How much more time did she need?

As Katie seemed to slip out of my life, someone else suddenly stepped back in. Out of nowhere I got a text from Andi. *Can we talk? I really miss you.*

I waited a while before answering. I honestly didn't know if I wanted to hear anything she had to say. Her dismissal of me still stung, and if she had been willing to drop me just because I had said I was bi, what was she going to think of me being trans? But when I told Mom, she said that Andi already knew. It turned out that her mom and mine had kept in touch this whole time.

"And Kelli is okay with me?" I asked, surprised.

"I think they've both come a long way," Mom said. "Give Andi a chance."

So I invited her over to go for a hike. It was unseasonably warm, and I was shocked when I opened the front door after the doorbell rang. It hadn't occurred to me that Andi would have changed—I guess I still expected to see the young-girl version of her, with long sleeves that she'd tug nervously around her hands to cover the skin, high-necked shirts, and shoulder-length hair that covered her face. Her hair was longer, and she wore it in a ponytail, revealing her sweet smile, and she was about three inches taller. But most shocking was her outfit—she was wearing denim shorts and a scoop neck T-shirt. Not deep enough to show cleavage or anything, but it was more skin than I'd ever seen on her. She looked like a totally normal teenage girl, full of confidence.

I realized that she was taking me in as well.

"You look great," she finally said.

"You too." I shut the door behind me and led her out back and onto the paths down into the woods. I still didn't know where this was going to go, and I wasn't ready to have her inside my house.

We scrambled onto the rocks and sat facing each other.

"Cool cabin," she said, pointing. "When did you build that?"

"Last year," I said, but inside I thought, *You should have been there with us.*

"Em . . . I mean Arin . . . ," she began, but stopped, embarrassed about almost calling me my birth name. I waited for her to recover.

"I never should have turned my back on you," she finally said.

"So why did you?" I asked.

"I saw things differently back then. I think it turns out we both did," she said with a smile.

I couldn't really argue with that, but I wasn't ready to give in.

"No, really. What made you change your mind? Do you still think I'm going to hell?"

She shook her head. "Hell isn't what religion should be about," she said. "It took me a while to figure it out, but I did. I really miss you. And I'm really, really proud of you for becoming who you are."

It meant everything to hear those words from her, but the rejection still weighed so heavily in my mind. I suppose it was because I finally had a real support system in place, and seeing her was a reminder of the really dark days when I hadn't. I knew that I needed to forgive her, but I also still needed a little time. And so that's what I told her.

I lasted about three days before I called her. "Don't ever ditch me again," I said.

"I won't," she promised. "I admit it—hearing about your becoming Arin confused me at first. A lot. But the more I thought about it, the more I think I always knew on some level. Even seeing you for the first time the other day, it was like looking at this ghost that I always sort of saw hovering over you when we were kids. Does that sound crazy?"

I felt a rush of love for her. "I've heard you say crazier things," I said, laughing. "I've *really* missed you."

• • •

The *Inside Edition* episode about Katie and me aired at the very end of October, and Andi came over to watch it with me. I thought the show was okay. It was a Disney version of us, for sure, but that was fine. They put such a flowers-and-rainbows spin on our lives that it relaxed me. There we were, cavorting around the yard and making moony eyes at each other. I guess I believed the hype. I didn't see Katie as much, but there we were on television, happy and in love. And in my mind that equaled our current state as well. It was still frustrating, though, to see all the images of us on the lake together, with her in a bikini and me totally covered up in a big shirt to hide my binder.

For some reason it hadn't really occurred to me that anyone would actually watch the show, but I got a flood of Facebook friend requests and messages after it aired. I was also nervous at school—no one came right up to me directly, but I thought I saw people staring at me more in the hallways. I kept my usual low profile, and at home I tried to answer everyone who wrote me, but there were so many new messages coming in that it got sort of overwhelming. But I continued to write back, remembering how much Skylarkeleven had helped me.

A few days later a bunch of blogs started to pick up the story. *America's First Teen Trans Couple!* one blared.

Well, that's just not true at all, I thought. I'd seen plenty of others at OYP and the Equality Center.

One night I was going through my Facebook messages, and I saw one from someone named Jamie. He introduced himself as a trans guy who hadn't started transitioning yet, and he wondered if I could suggest any good gender therapists in the Tulsa area. I checked out his profile and saw that he went to a high school the next town over!

I wrote him back immediately and told him that we should meet up, and that I could point him in the direction of lots of resources.

We agreed to meet after school on a Friday, at a coffee shop that was in between our two schools. I waited outside for about fifteen minutes and was just starting to wonder if I'd been stood up, when I noticed a tall, skinny guy standing a few feet away from me, with long curly brown hair that hung in his face.

"Jamie?" I asked.

"Hey," he said meekly.

He looked so nervous, and I felt an immediate connection to him. I'd been where he was now. I pictured how happy I would have been if Skylarkeleven had magically jumped out of the computer screen and personally guided me through my own transition, and I became determined to help Jamie in any way I could.

"Let's go inside and talk," I said.

He was painfully shy at first, and would barely look me in the eye. Getting any information from him was hard, but I managed to learn that he was a senior and headed to college in Tennessee the following year, and he wanted to enter transitioned.

I told him all about Taylor Burns and gave Jamie his number, along with mine.

"Call me any time you need to talk," I said. "I know how hard it is, but Taylor is great, and you're going to be fine."

We met up again about a week later at the same spot, but I didn't recognize him when he came up to me, because he had cut all his hair off. He had a really kind smile, and freckles that I hadn't noticed before.

"You look amazing!" I said.

"Thanks!" he said. "I made an appointment with your therapist. I'm seeing him next week!"

A friend of my family's was throwing a huge bonfire party that weekend, and I invited Jamie to come along. He balked at first. It seemed like he didn't want to impose, but I badgered him, and he finally agreed.

It was mid-December at this point and I'd just gotten my driver's license, so I picked him up to bring him to the party. He was still acting really shy and quiet, no matter how many questions I asked him. On the way to the party, we had to pass through Claremore, the small town closest to Papa and Gigi. As I neared the town border, I saw a blockade set up and a bunch of cops on the corner. One of them waved me over, so I rolled down the window.

"Evening, officer," I said. "What's up?"

"It's the Christmas parade," he said. "We just shut down Main Street. You'll need to take a detour."

"Oh, man. We're already really late for this thing we need to get to. Are you sure you can't let us through? It doesn't look like they've even started yet. Please?"

I pointed to a side street where I could see a bunch of floats, and people dressed as Santa's elves scurrying around.

"Oh, let 'em through," another cop called. "He's right. They need a few more minutes."

The policeman sighed and moved the barricade, waving us through. We drove about a block and turned to the center of town, where the sidewalks were packed with what looked like every single resident. As soon as they saw my car, a huge *whoop* went up from the crowd, and everyone started screaming and waving.

"What the hell?" Jamie said, slinking down in his seat.

"Oh, man. They think we're the start of the parade," I said, and laughed. "Just go with it." I slowed to a crawl, rolled down my window, and stuck an arm out, yelling, "Merry Christmas, everyone!"

Jamie looked like he wanted to die. "Come on," I urged him.

He sat up a little and smiled, and rolled down his window. "Merry Christmas," he called out faintly.

"Louder!" I started honking my horn, and the crowd kept cheering.

"Meeerrry Christmaaasss!" Jamie shouted, and we both cracked up and tore out of town.

We became really close after that. We even call that night our friend anniversary. The only problem was that he didn't like Katie. I introduced them right after Jamie and I started hanging out, and even though he denied it when I brought it up, I got the distinct vibe that he didn't trust her. It was nothing he said—he'd just get kind of quiet whenever she was around.

I still saw Katie on the weekends, but sometimes it was

every other weekend. She was busy keeping her grades where they needed to be in order to stay in school. But she promised to spend the holidays with my family.

I couldn't wait for winter break to begin. Gigi sewed Katie a stocking so she would feel included on Christmas morning. The day was so much fun, everyone laughing and tossing gifts at one another, and we stuffed our faces with ham, scalloped potatoes—and hot apple pie for dessert. Everything felt back to normal, but the day after, my mouth began to ache horribly. I tried to ignore it at first, thinking that maybe I had just been grinding my teeth at night, but the pain became so unbearable that Mom took me to the dentist.

"Your wisdom teeth are infected," he told me after poking around in my mouth. "They need to be removed immediately."

I couldn't have *surgery*. This was my Katie time!

The doctor assured me that I'd be laid up for only a few days, but the recovery period lasted two weeks. My entire head felt like it was on fire, and I had to take painkillers. They made me groggy and cranky, and I was in a horrible mood all the time. I wanted to be outside sledding with Katie and going on dates—having the equivalent of our magic summer but in the chilly beauty of the snow. I wanted to snuggle up with her next to an outdoor fire, catch snowflakes on our tongues, and ice-skate while holding hands.

But the only thing I had the energy for was sitting in bed and staring at the television. And even though she stayed by my side, things weren't the same between us. I was comfortable enough with her by that point to sleep without a shirt or binder on and be completely physically naked, but emotionally we were starting to disconnect. We began to get into big arguments over the stupidest little things, like the proper definition of the phrase "empty calorie." (I was right.)

School started back up just as my mouth was starting to feel better, but I'd missed out on my chance to rekindle the magic between us. Katie disappeared back into her college world again, and I spent the rest of the winter having to be content with the occasional weekend visits. Mom knew how upset I was about missing out on my chance to spend quality time with Katie, so for spring break she offered to take us and my friends Jamie and Tim skiing in Colorado. I love to ski and hardly ever get the chance to.

Katie didn't seem as excited about the prospect when I invited her, but I knew she was dealing with midterms, so I chalked her indifference up to distraction.

The day after her last test, we all piled into Mom's car and drove for nine hours, with Wes in the front seat controlling the stereo and trying to impress us with his considerable belching skills.

By the time we arrived, I was desperate to get out into clean air, but we had to wait until morning to get to the top of the mountain. When we jumped off the ski lift, I pulled Katie aside and into the tree line, away from the crowds. The entire world stretched out behind her—snowcapped peaks and a sky so blue, it almost hurt my eyes. The cheers and screams of people disappearing down the slopes seemed to simply fade away, until it was just the two of us, on top of our own private mountain.

"I got you something," I said. "I know things have been a little off between us, and I know how hard you're working at school. I just want you to know that I'm always, always here for you."

I pulled a ring out of my coat pocket, where I'd been clutching it nervously. It was just a simple band. I couldn't afford silver, so I'd chosen tungsten because it's supposed to never scratch or bend.

"It's a promise ring. Not like in an 'I want to marry you someday' way, but just so you know that I promise I will always be true to you."

She got this sad look in her eye for a split second before putting it on. "It's beautiful," she said. "Thank you."

We were getting ready to head down the first slope, when out of nowhere Katie suddenly fell and hurt her foot.

"I think I need to go back to the lodge," she said.

I was a little bummed, but more concerned about her. "Come on. I'll escort you down," I told her. She could still stand and ski, so we made our way slowly down a side slope. But when we got to the bottom, she freaked out.

"You weren't watching me at all!" she yelled. "You should have been watching out for me, and you just took off!"

I blinked. Maybe I'd gotten caught up in the thrill a couple of times, but I had always kept my eye on her to make sure she was okay. I stammered an apology and walked her back to the room, where I got her settled on the couch with the television remote and some hot chocolate.

I started to put my coat back on. "Where are you going?" she asked.

"Back out . . . ," I said, my voice trailing off as I realized that was not the answer she wanted to hear.

"You're not going to stay here with me?"

"I mean, we came here to ski, and your foot is okay, and it's totally cool if you just want to hang back. . . ." I was making it worse with every word.

"Go," she said, flipping on the TV.

"Katie . . ."

"No, just go. Have fun."

And so I went. I can see now how it was kind of a jerk move, but we'd spent so much money to go all the way out there to ski, something I never got to do. And it wasn't like she'd broken her leg or anything. It wasn't even a sprain.

Those were all the things I kept telling myself on the ride back up the mountain, but a week after we got back, she told me that she wanted to break up.

16

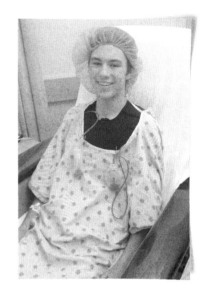

We were hanging out at Papa and Gigi's, just watching TV. I put a bottle of root beer in the fridge to get cold. I went to the bathroom, came back, and saw Katie drinking the soda.

"Really?" I teased. "I just put that in there for myself!"

When we got into the car to drive home, I heard her inhale deeply and then let it all out in a huge sigh.

Oh no, I thought.

"You're so selfish and mean," she cried. "This isn't working anymore!" She handed me the ring I'd given her. "Here. You're not ready for something like this. You don't make me feel loved."

The only thing I *lived* for was to make her feel loved!

"Katie, we-we've got to talk about this," I managed to stammer. I was thoroughly freaking out. "We can't just throw away what we have!"

I convinced her to come back to my house so we could talk about it, and the whole way over she rattled off a list of all the ways I was mean to her. But none of it made sense.

She asked for her space because of school, and so I gave it to her. And when we were together, I doted on her. She seemed desperate to cling to the ski trip as an example of our entire relationship. I felt like I was going crazy. Was I an asshole and just didn't know it? I was pretty sure I wasn't. Maybe testosterone was having an even bigger effect on me than I'd realized.

By the time we got to the house, I was so worked up that I punched the garage door. Which probably didn't do anything for my image as a jerk in her eyes.

"Please," I begged her. "We've got to work through this. We can't just ditch it. I'll do whatever you need me to. I'll keep the ring. I can give it back when the time is right."

After a deluge of promises and tears, she agreed to stay with me. But it was never really the same after that. I saw less and less of her, as she often broke dates. When we did hang out, she talked a lot about her college friends, new ones that I'd never met. She kept the two halves of her life separate. There was college Katie, and my girlfriend Katie.

The main thing that kept me going for the rest of my junior year was that I was scheduled to have my top surgery as soon as the school year was over. I'd been living as a guy for a year, and Mom had finally agreed to let me have the surgery. After that I'd have the entire summer to finally be in at least half of my true body with Katie. We could rekindle what we'd had before, after all the pressures of her first year of college were gone.

I had a suspicion, though, that maybe one of the reasons Katie was withdrawing was because she finally had the body she was meant to have, and therefore she no longer needed my support and companionship. But I buried that thought whenever it came up. I was just projecting my own insecurity. When we were together, and not fighting, she always told me how much she loved me.

My surgery was nowhere near the level of Katie's. Since my breasts were a small B cup, I was just on the border of being eligible for something called full keyhole surgery. If your breasts are any larger, you need to get a bilateral mastectomy, which can leave significant scarring. But with keyhole surgery a surgeon simply makes an incision around your nipple and pulls the tissue out through the hole, and uses liposuction to remove the rest of the fat out through your armpits. If the doctors need to, they resize the areola to make it smaller so it matches your new flat chest, but mine were small enough to begin with, so they didn't need to change them. Keyhole surgery leaves virtually no scars, and it isn't supposed to affect nipple sensation. And since I was so young, it would be much easier for my skin to snap back into place and adhere to the pectoral muscles without any stretch marks.

Taylor had recommended a few surgeons to us, but they all charged between ten thousand and twelve thousand dollars, and there was no way I could afford that. So I did a lot of Internet research and found a doctor in Cleveland who charged only sixty-five hundred dollars. Not that sixty-five hundred dollars is cheap, but I was able to save part of the money myself through working at Danco, and Mom agreed to pay for the rest. I don't take this lightly. I know that there are so many transgender people out there who can't afford any kind of surgery, and I'm beyond grateful that I have a family willing to help me financially.

Katie wasn't able to come see me off, because she had a final that day, but she sent me a ton of *Good luck* and *I love you* texts. As I was getting into the car to head to the airport, Wes came running up to me in the driveway.

"Listen," he said. "Since this is the last time you're ever going to have boobs, can I touch them?"

"Fine," I said, and sighed.

He reached up and squeezed them, making a *honk, honk* sound before cracking up and giving me a huge hug. "Come home soon," he said, suddenly getting all quiet and serious. "I love you."

After we landed, we checked into a one-bedroom suite in a hotel near the hospital. Aunt Susan and Gigi had come along with us, and I shared the main bed with Mom and Susan, while Gigi stayed on a foldout sofa in the living room.

That night Mom and I went downstairs to the hotel hot tub. I wore my binder under a tank top, barely able to comprehend that it was the last time I would ever have to feel self-conscious about my chest. The double layers of fabric felt even tighter than usual because of all the steam, but I didn't care—the joy of knowing that my breasts would be gone by that same time tomorrow more than made up for any discomfort.

We sat in the tub not talking, mist swirling up around us. I knew what kind of thoughts must have been running through my mom's mind, and I didn't want to interrupt the moment for her. Even though she was happy for me, I knew a part of her was grieving, that the finality of it all must have been fully hitting her. I wanted her to have this time of quiet reflection with me still in the physical body she had given birth to, rather than her having to hear me gloat about how psyched I was. It was still hard for me to fathom how far we'd come together, and it meant everything to me that this was all happening with her blessing.

The surgery was an outpatient procedure, and we arrived at the hospital at noon. In the prep room Susan kept making jokes about breasts, bouncing hers up and down and drawing smiley faces on her arms using the surgery marker. "You're cutting your boobs off. Come on, let's have some fun," she said, laughing as the nurses shot disapproving looks our way. I knew it was just her way of masking how scared she was that I was going into surgery.

As the nurses got ready to wheel me off, Mom's eyes started to tear up. She kissed me good-bye and told me she loved me.

"Ready?" the doctor asked when I arrived inside the operating room.

"Ready," I said, and the anesthesiologist lowered the mask over my face and asked me to count back from ten. The last thing I remember thinking is, *It's not real.*

The second I awoke, I stuck my head up and looked at my chest. There was nothing there except a tight black surgical-grade binder to keep everything compressed. The room suddenly started to spin, and I dropped my head back down. *It happened,* I thought. Mom appeared by the stretcher.

"How are you feeling?" she asked.

I struggled to get words out of my mouth. "Loopy," I managed to slur. "I got morphine." There was no pain, and it actually felt sort of amazing. I turned my head and saw a camera in my face. I'd forgotten that we'd agreed to let *Inside Edition* film the surgery. I closed my eyes and let the world fall away.

I stayed in the hospital for the rest of the afternoon for monitoring, and then got sent home to the hotel. There were two drain tubes sticking out of my armpits for extra fluid to pour out of—a sort of thin, watery blood that collected in little bags I called blood grenades. They needed to be emptied constantly.

Mom stayed by my bedside, feeding me Percocet so that I could get through the pain. I couldn't even raise a glass to my lips to drink water, so she ran out and bought bendy straws to hold up to my mouth. My arms were utterly useless, and she even had to pull my pants down for me the first time I needed to go to the bathroom. Gigi and Susan left after the first two days, and by the third, Mom and I were going stir-crazy. We watched a never-ending feast of cooking shows on cable, but it did nothing to help me work up an appetite. I pretty much lived on ice cream and soup. The painkillers made me feel good for a little while, but soon they started to make me feel nauseous and cloudy. I wanted my clear thoughts back, but more than anything, I wanted to see my new chest. The binder had to stay on for five full days, though. A barrage of text messages from Jamie and Andi and my cousins sending their love helped stem the boredom. Toward the end of the stay, I finally felt strong enough to actually leave the hotel. Mom and I went to a nearby restaurant and were so psyched to be around other people. We felt like tourists in an alien world, after being cooped up with just each other for so long.

The day before we left, we went back to the hospital to have my bandages removed. As the nurse unwound the wrap, I glanced down. My nipples were scabbed over and there were still incisions healing from where the tubes had gone into my pits, but other than that, it was perfect. It was like looking down the sheer side of a cliff. The nurse brought over a mirror.

I was finally looking at myself—the person I always saw when I closed my eyes. I was wearing my soul on my skin for the first time in my life.

I was insanely happy, but there was also a sort of calm that settled over me, a peaceful feeling of relief. It was similar to the sensation I got after finally cutting my hair off, but magnified times a million. My shoulders were still bent from years of hunching over to hide my chest, and I tried to straighten my posture. Pain shot through me, so I let my shoulders release back to their normal position. But not before I took a quick selfie.

Everyone back home kept texting and asking me to send them photos, but I wrote that I wanted to show everyone at once when we returned.

I showered carefully as soon as we got back to the hotel,

cleansing away a week's worth of sweat off my chest. It felt so wonderfully strange to soap up the area, no longer encumbered by the two mounds that had gotten in the way for the past six years. I had flashes of being a child, remembering how normal it had felt to shower, back when there had never been anything there to begin with.

When I was done showering, I walked back into the bedroom to grab some clothes. Mom was sitting on the bed, and she gave me a funny look.

"You know you don't have to do that anymore, right?" she asked.

I was confused until I followed her gaze and glanced down. Out of sheer habit I had wrapped my towel around my entire upper body.

"Oh yeah!" I said. I let the towel drop down to my waist and sauntered casually across the room, relishing every second.

Early the next morning, as our plane sped down the runway, I felt so strongly that I was leaving a part of me behind. I suppose because it was true. Some people leave their hearts in San Francisco; I left my tits in Cleveland.

The entire ride home I stared at the photo I'd taken of myself on my phone. A whole new chapter of my life was about to start—shirtless Arin. I could finally have sex with Katie without worrying that my breasts were going to flop around. When we landed, she was waiting, along with Amanda and Cheyenne. Aside from texting, Katie and I had barely spoken the entire time I'd been gone, but I'd been too excited about the surgery to really notice. Amanda gave me a homemade notebook called *50 Reasons Why You Are Awesome*, with exactly that—fifty cards with beautiful little compliments written on them.

We drove to my dad's for the big reveal. I needed some help getting my shirt off, and turned my back to the room while Mom helped me undo the binder.

I spun around.

Everyone whistled and cheered. And then Cheyenne said, "Your nipples are *really* black."

"They'll heal," I answered.

Katie met me back at my house, and we went upstairs so I could show her my chest.

"It looks incredible," she told me, reaching out and gently touching it.

I told her all about the surgery, and we compared our spaced-out morphine experiences.

"Get into bed with me," I said. I was still in too much pain to attempt to have sex, but she didn't seem especially eager to anyway, so we just stretched out side by side and flipped on the TV. She stayed over that night but spent most of the time texting someone on her phone. I fell asleep early, exhausted and emotionally spent.

17

Over the next week, I still needed help with normal things like getting milk out of the refrigerator. The full recovery time is six weeks, and you aren't supposed to do any sort of heavy lifting for twelve, which meant the whole summer. For the first few weeks all I did was sit around and watch a lot of TV. I was pretty boring to be around, so I didn't blame Katie for not coming around as much. And anytime I started to get nervous about us, she assured me in her texts that everything was fine, per usual.

I needed to line up a summer job. Doing something in the warehouse at Danco would have been the first choice, but I couldn't because of all the physical exertion it required.

I ended up getting hired to make tamales out of a wagon run by a local restaurant called Molly's Landing. They kept it parked next to the giant blue whale of Catoosa, one of the most famous roadside attractions on Route 66. The story goes that back in the 1970s some rich guy had a wife who was obsessed with collecting whale figurines, so he built her a giant whale next to a pond on their property. It has a huge open mouth that you can walk into, a slide coming out of its belly that goes into the water, and a ladder that leads up to a little viewing platform at the tip of its tail. Kids used to sneak onto their property to play on it, so he eventually opened it up to the public and built a little beach. Today you aren't allowed to swim in the pond, but the whale itself still gets plenty of visitors—a lot of overseas tourists doing the fabled Route 66 road trip across America. So I started to spend my days passing out tamales to a never-ending caravan of fussy Brits and unimpressed Germans.

During this entire time the original media company that had contacted me and Katie was visiting and filming every few weeks because they wanted to put together a reel for a possible documentary about Katie and me. *20/20* came to do a special on us too, so whenever the camera crews arrived, Katie dutifully came over and got dressed up, and we played our parts. We had the role of the all-American teen trans couple down to a science at that point.

I understood why the cameras liked us so much. We were safe for the masses—white, telegenic, and heteronormative. It bothered me that no one was interested in filming any of the other trans teens at OYP so that we could represent a broader spectrum of our local community, but I told myself that we were at least helping to get the conversation started on a larger scale.

The other problem was that the only time I felt like Katie and I were in an actual relationship was when the cameras were rolling. She'd become super-affectionate and laugh and tease and kiss me, but as soon as everyone packed up, she'd disappear too. She continued to assure me that everything was fine between us, but we barely ever fooled around anymore. It bothered me of course—hell, I was a horny teenage guy—but at the same time the emotional distance between us made the physical desire lessen. The best part of sex with her had always been the emotional closeness. And in a weird way I missed Katie's old body, when we'd both had the wrong genitals but had been matched up in our minds. We had been on an even playing field before, but now she had not only surpassed me, but she also seemed anxious to make the distance even wider.

As summer neared its end and I became completely healed, I started hitting the gym really hard. Now that I had my chest taken care of, I wanted to start shaping the rest of my body. I could grow a full chin strap of hair by then, but I still had hips, sort of an hourglass figure, and the only way to get rid of that is to add bulk and muscle to the torso so it fills out the sides. My metabolism is out of control, though. I can eat, like, a gazillion calories a day and not gain a pound. I started drinking protein shakes and installed a pull-up bar in my bedroom doorframe to bulk up my pecs. I've always had abs, even as a little kid, so they weren't hard to start toning more. It's not like I want to look like some totally ripped tool, but I'd already undergone major surgery to get the body I wanted. I owed it to myself to keep it healthy. And, to be perfectly honest, I hoped that if I looked manlier, then maybe Katie would start showing more interest in me. But as had become her habit, she got really invested in hanging out only when a media opportunity arose.

Right as school was starting, we got a call from the *Trisha Goddard* show, asking us to appear on it. I'd never heard of the program, but I got excited. The producers were offering to fly us to Stamford, Connecticut, where the show shoots, and our moms both agreed that we should all stay on in New York City for a few days afterward, since we were going to be so close. I figured it would be a great opportunity for Katie and me to have a romantic getaway.

Everything was great at first. We cuddled up against each other once we were settled on the plane, and I carried her bags for her through the terminal when we landed. We spent the first day shooting random footage of us wandering around outside in the grass, playing the carefree couple. It all went great, and we were given vouchers for free dinners that night at our fancy hotel. As soon as we got into the car service to head to the hotel, Katie started acting distracted again. She was glued to her phone, sending text after text after text. When I asked her about it, she said, "Oh, it's just my friend Todd. He's been helping me study for this one exam."

Todd. I'd heard her mention the name before. When we got to the hotel, I snuck off to the bathroom and went onto Facebook on my phone, searching her friends for someone named Todd. There was one guy, but every time I tried to click on him, I got an error message that said, *page not found*. I figured it was a reception problem.

When we started to get ready to head downstairs to dinner, Katie begged off.

"I'm so tired, and not really hungry," she said. "I'm just going to stay up here."

We tried to convince her to come down with us, but she kept insisting, so we told her we'd bring some food back up for her later. Jazzlyn seemed embarrassed when we got to our table.

"She's just really been under a lot of stress lately," she said.

The next morning we woke up crazy early to get to the *Trisha Goddard* show, and it was basically a disaster. If you watch the clips online, you can tell that our body language is drastically different from anything we'd filmed previously. Part of the problem was that our relationship was crumbling, but the other issue—which you can't tell by the edit—was that one of the very first things the show's host asked us was how we have sex. We were both startled. I genuinely understand the curiosity, but in front of an audience of strangers, it felt like a sneak attack. Not to mention that I was a minor at the time.

In the right forum and context, I'm okay now with discussing sex and my own genital dysphoria, but it's *really* important to understand that many trans people aren't. And it sucks when that's the first thing a stranger asks about. Any topic relating to bodies, sex, and sexuality is going to be different for everyone, and privacy should be respected.

We dodged the question and ran through all of our normal lines, but I couldn't wait for the interview to end so we could get out of there.

The producers provided us with car service to New York City, and we checked into our new hotel in midtown just as the sun was starting to set. Mom suggested we go to the Empire State Building, and Katie jumped up.

"Yes!" she said. "Let's get out of here, go see the city!"

Outside, it was a perfect New York evening. There was a clean, brisk breeze that seemed to sweep all the grime from the city. I inhaled the smell of honey-roasted peanuts wafting from a street vendor standing on the corner. Everything around me felt alive and huge. I buried all my frustrations about the show taping and all my worries about Katie's friend Todd. I was determined to have a beautiful night out with my girlfriend. I turned to reach for Katie's hand.

But she wasn't there.

Confused, I looked around and saw her taking off, at least five steps ahead of me. "Hey, wait up," I called, but she either ignored me or didn't hear. I started to speed up, but Jazzlyn and Mom were on either side of me, asking me questions about what else I wanted to do for the rest of our trip.

Fix my relationship, I thought while desperately praying that Katie would turn around, see that we'd fallen behind, and wait for us. But she didn't, so I ran to catch up with her.

"Hey," I said, breathless by the time I reached her side. "Wait up!"

"Oh, sorry. I just love New York. It makes me excited. I guess I walk faster here." She laughed and then stopped abruptly as she started texting again, glancing up every few seconds so that she didn't ram into anyone. Since her hands were occupied, I couldn't try to hold one. I slowed my pace until I was back in line with Mom and Jazzlyn.

Turn around, I silently pleaded to Katie's rapidly disappearing back.

When we got to the top of the Empire State Building, I

hoped that some of its legendary charm would rub off on Katie, but she kept running from one platform to the next while I followed miserably behind. I'd been fantasizing about kissing her with all of Manhattan stretched out before us as a witness. She eventually gave me a little peck, but for the most part the closest I got to her lips was a view of them glowing in the light of her cell phone.

I pulled out my own and texted Jamie, who was just getting settled into college in Tennessee.

I think Katie hates me.

Why, what's up?

She's just acting really weird. Can you look into a guy named Todd for me? She's friends with him on Facebook, but I can't access his page for some reason.

On it.

Things got a little better once we returned to the hotel. Katie finally put away her phone and climbed between Mom and me on one of the room's beds, and rested her head on my chest while I flipped through the TV channels, looking for something to watch. Jazzlyn lay on the other bed, dozing. I stroked Katie's hair, wondering yet again if I was just being paranoid about her.

My phone started vibrating. It was Jamie calling. I answered quickly so I wouldn't disturb Katie.

"What's up?" I whispered.

"I didn't want to text this to you. Arin, I found this guy's Facebook page. There's all this stuff on there about how he and Katie are dating. And it goes way back, like since before the summer."

I felt the strangest chill run through my entire body, like adrenaline, only a thousand times more intense. It was like there was ice in my veins, and my head started buzzing. I suddenly couldn't breathe.

"She's sleeping on my chest."

"She's playing you," he said. "I'm so sorry."

"I gotta go," I said, and hung up.

"Hey," I said, slipping out from under her. She opened her eyes and looked up at me. "Can I talk to you out in the hall for a sec?" I asked, keeping my voice calm.

"Sure," she said, stretching her arms above her head and yawning.

I lit into her the second we got into the hall. And she denied it all.

"I've grown really close to him emotionally," she said. "That's it! I've never even kissed him! I'm with you!"

"Why would he say on Facebook that he's dating you, when it says on our pages that we're together?" I asked, genuinely confused. I wanted so bad to believe her. "He's posting about it to all his friends, and has been for *months* apparently!"

"How . . . I mean, why were you even looking at his page?" she asked.

"Because he's all you talk about!" I yelled.

"Look at me," she said, grabbing my head and staring me in the eyes. "There is nothing between us. He is just a friend, and nothing has ever happened. And I'm sorry if I'm distracted, but college is really intense, so much more than high school ever was. I *swear* that you're the only one. I hang out with Todd at school a lot, and he's probably just referring to that."

"You need to fix this," I said. "We just went on national TV and talked about how in love we are!"

"We are in love!" she said.

"I know *I* am," I said.

"And I am too. I'll talk to Todd and tell him to cool it. It's all going to be fine."

But it wasn't. The rest of the trip was so awkward, and I couldn't wait to get home. The four of us were all crammed into one tiny hotel room together, and I didn't get a chance to tell Mom what was going on until we were out sightseeing and Katie and Jazzlyn wandered off for a moment. She was livid but understood that I wanted to give Katie a chance to make things right.

I kept my head down everywhere we went. I became obsessed with all the weird black dots on the sidewalks, until I realized that they were wads of chewing gum that had been trampled so much that they'd turned black with the filth of the city. That's how the trip felt to me—I'd shown up all pink and happy and bubbly, and now I'd been spit out and stomped on. New York suddenly seemed cold and impersonal. I went through the motions of a vacation—snapping all the requisite photos, but I was totally numb inside. By the time we left, Katie and I were barely speaking. We didn't say a word on the plane ride home. I still carried her bags through the airport when we landed, but she didn't thank me. I went to give her a hug, but she kept her arms by her side.

Mom drove me to a restaurant where we had arranged to meet Jamie, who had driven back from Tennessee to console me. But I wasn't hungry, so I told Mom I'd just ride home with Jamie instead. In his car he offered up a bottle of sweet tea and some jerky he'd bought to cheer me up.

"So, what are you gonna do?" he asked as I took a swig of the drink.

"She says there's nothing going on, and I have to trust her. I love her. She told me she's going to get this Todd guy to stop posting stuff about her and break off the friendship."

"Well, I'm here for you. I can always drive to visit on the weekends."

Two days later I got a Facebook message:

Hey, Arin. You don't know me, but my name is Todd. I'm not sure why your Facebook page says that you're dating Katie Hill. She's my girlfriend.

18

I drove straight to Katie's dorm, even though she begged me not to. "I don't want to see you. Let's just do this over the phone," she pleaded when I called her. But I told her I was coming no matter what, and she was waiting for me outside her building. Her arms were folded tight against her, and she wouldn't look up.

I didn't want to have the conversation we were about to have in public, so I drove us to my dad's house, since I knew he would be at work. We sat down on his sofa, and I had a memory flash of Wes busting Darian and me making out on it. I smiled sadly. That part of my life felt like it was a million years ago.

"Why are you doing this?" I asked. "Why did you lie?"

"It's weird," she said softly. "I feel like a black widow spider, like I just want to keep drawing all these men into my web."

"What the hell does that mean?" I freaked. "Have there been others?"

She finally turned to face me. "No," she said. "But Todd makes me feel like a woman. I need a man with a real penis."

There was a momentary blackness.

I was utterly destroyed.

It was the one tool I didn't have in my kit to try to fix this. I could profess my undying love for her, promise to change anything about my personality that she didn't like, even give her more time apart so she could have some breathing room. But I couldn't grow a cis penis.

She was the one who was supposed to understand. I had opened my mind *and* body to her—it was a double betrayal. She was telling me I wasn't man enough for her. I could never in a trillion years fathom telling her, even before her surgery, that she wasn't woman enough.

I tried to take normal breaths as she told me that she had been secretly dating Todd for several months now. She wasn't physically attracted to me anymore, and hadn't been for a long time. Now that she had a female body, she wanted to experience it with a cis guy.

"But I still love you," I cried.

"I still love you, too," she told me. "And I think maybe someday I even want to end up back with you. But I need to experience my life now, on my own terms."

That was the cruelest twist. She was dangling a piece of her so-called web to keep me wrapped up in her life. And I was in love, so there was nothing I could do but take the tiny, pathetic piece of hope she had to offer.

It would have been kinder for her to say that she hated me and never wanted to see me again.

• • •

When I got home, I went straight into the woods out back. I walked down to the cabin on the rocks and crawled inside to think, to process that my life as I knew it had just crumbled down around me. But the confining space didn't feel right. I needed to be out in the air, in the open, to clear my head.

I needed to build something new.

There were some old materials left over from the cabin's construction, so I dragged four beams and a flat piece of compressed wood farther down the hill on the other side of the house, to a small space between two trees with branches that didn't obscure the view of the sky. I dug holes, hammered nails, and by twilight I had a tall platform that rose about six feet off the ground, affixed to one side of a tree.

Fall was coming on fast, and I even though I'd just built it, I had to sweep a few leaves off the surface when I climbed up and stretched out on my back.

As the stars came out one by one, I wondered if this was some sort of karmic revenge for the way I'd handled my breakup with Darian.

19

I was numb over the next several weeks. I went to school, worked at the tamale stand in the afternoons, hit the gym in the evenings, and did my homework before bed. *Just go through the motions of a normal life,* I told myself. I wasn't purposely trying to bury the pain—I think I was in such a state of shock that my brain automatically did that for me.

Any efforts to try to break myself out of that haze—like hiking in the woods or going out swing dancing—ended with my sitting and staring off into space. By the time I started feeling emotions again, the dominating one was self-loathing because I didn't have the equipment Katie wanted. I told myself that, rationally, it made sense for her to feel the way she did, but my heart refused to listen to what my head was trying to tell it. Katie and I still texted and hung out every now and then, but it was so scarily easy to fall back into our old routine of being affectionate that I'd find myself forgetting we'd even broken up, and when we'd say good-bye, I'd come crashing back to reality.

Jamie drove from college to visit me every weekend and force me out of the house, and little by little I started to feel like myself again. One day, when we had fallen down a YouTube hole of prank videos that had us cracking up, I got a message on Facebook from a casting director asking if I wanted to be in a photo shoot for some store called Barneys. I'd never heard of it. They offered to fly me up to New York for a few days to model a bunch of clothes with other trans people.

"Who the hell is Bruce Weber?" I asked Jamie when I read the photographer's name. He shrugged. I did a Google search, and more than ten million hits popped up.

"Damn," I said.

Turned out he was a pretty big deal. There were a lot of black-and-white photos of half-naked people, and he had taken pictures of tons of celebrities for fancy magazines such as *Vogue* and *Vanity Fair*.

I didn't want to go, though. I'd grown accustomed to my routine and felt pretty much done with being on camera. I was still wincing over a painful segment Katie and I had ended up shooting. The segment producers had heard that we had broken up and had convinced us that people would want to know. So Katie and I did a series of awkwardly staged interviews where we did ridiculous things like hold hands, but then slowly drift apart as we walked down my street. It was humiliating, especially because I couldn't say the *real* reason we'd broken up—that she'd been cheating on me with another guy. Instead it was all about us "being in different places" and "staying friends." I wanted to scream the truth into the camera, but I didn't want to make Katie look or feel bad.

My mom eventually convinced me that the Barneys shoot would be really good for trans visibility. I told Bruce Weber's people all about Katie, and they ended up hiring her, too. Before I knew it, we were planning yet another trip to New York City. I prayed that this one would go better than the previous one.

Mom and Aunt Susan came with us as our chaperones. The shoot was . . . I guess the only way to describe it is unreal. I felt like I was living inside a movie. The first day of shooting took place in Central Park, and it seemed like there were hundreds of assistants and hair and makeup people running through the trees. There were giant trailers set up, and inside them we tried on thousands and thousands of dollars' worth of clothes, before heading outside to be photographed and gawked at by tourists. There were fifteen other trans people, and only a few had ever modeled professionally before. It was a whirlwind three-day trip, full of camera flashes and fashion and fancy dinners. On the last afternoon, as we were shooting inside a huge studio with a sick view of the Manhattan skyline and an assistant was applying dirt smears on my face for what I guess was a sort of chimney-sweep/street-urchin look, I wondered how the hell I'd gotten there. How *all* of us had gotten there. Life was moving so fast.

Things were cool with Katie during the trip. I was getting more and more used to the idea of us being friends, even though we still cuddled constantly. By the time we flew back home, I felt like I was almost over losing her. My heart didn't hurt as bad, and I wondered if the lessening pain might have had something to do with being in New York and seeing just how much more there is to life. Hearing all the other models' stories helped bring me out of my head—I realized once more just how lucky I had it compared to so many others, in terms of my family and support system. Case in point: I hadn't heard from Dale in a long time, but right after I returned, I received a text from him. He'd attempted suicide and had just been released from a hospital. Just as he'd feared, his family had turned their backs on him when he'd come out as trans. We made plans to meet up, and I was determined to do everything in my power to help him pull through. I wanted—I *needed*—to do anything I could to try to help people who were going through what I went through, or worse.

Just after New Year's Day, I was asked to speak on a trans awareness panel at Northeastern State University, about an hour east of Tulsa. Afterward, as I was getting ready to leave, I saw a really tall guy come walking through the crowd toward me. He looked familiar, and when his face suddenly scrunched up into a nervous half smile, I realized it was Austin, the guy whom I'd friend requested on Facebook almost three years before, right before the spring break cruise. The one who had ignored me after I'd told him I was trans. I'd actually seen him in person a few times at OYP, but we'd always avoided each other in that awkward way that you do when you know someone only through the Internet instead of real life.

"Hi," he said, playing with his hands and then suddenly shoving them both behind his back and rocking back and forth on his feet. His eyes darted warily up to the ceiling, as if a giant hand might drop down and carry him away. His hair was still blond, but it wasn't spiky anymore. It was smoothed out. I had a weird urge to reach up and ruffle it to help calm him down. "So, I, uh, came to this."

"Yeah, I can see," I said.

"Do you want to maybe get some coffee or something?" he asked.

"Sure," I said.

We drove in our separate cars to a Starbucks, got drinks, and sat down.

"So, um, I want to apologize for sort of blowing you off when you first reached out to me. I was a lot younger, and I think it kind of freaked me out."

"No problem," I said. "I don't really remember what I was doing. I just thought you were cute."

"So you're gay?" he asked.

The question sort of startled me. No one had asked me that in forever, and I wasn't even sure how to answer. I was attracted to him, but that was the point—I was attracted to *him*. Not guys in general. Or girls in general. I think what I feel now is something separate from even bisexual.

"I don't really think in terms like that anymore," I said. "I mean, I definitely thought you were cute when I first saw a picture of you, but now I understand that I'm attracted to a person's spirit first, then their body. And by that time it doesn't matter what that body is. Does that make sense?"

He nodded. "Totally. I'm gay, but I think I'm sort of gender neutral. Like, I know the outside of my body is a boy, and I'm happy with that. But inside I'm something else, at least in terms of how society expects a boy should be. I just happen to be stuck in a form that represents something different to the outside world from what I feel in my soul."

I totally understood, and I felt my heart speed up a little. We talked for a while longer. He told me he was from a tiny town nearby outside of Muskogee, and he was a freshman at a local college, studying to be a nurse practitioner.

"I like the idea of helping to heal people," he said.

He had read stuff about Katie and me in the news, and I told him the truth behind all the stories about us.

"I'm really sorry you got hurt so bad," he said.

"Thanks. We're always going to have a connection, but I'm really starting to come out of it now."

It was getting late, and I had to get back home, so we said good-bye and promised to stay in touch. I felt giddy the whole drive back.

We texted back and forth over the next month, and each message I got from him made me like him a little bit more. He was so self-deprecating and funny and smart—veering from a rant against the death penalty one moment to moaning about his chocolate addiction the next. But I kept my mouth shut about my feelings. I didn't want to mess up our new friendship, so I just joked around and kept him up to date about random things happening in my life—and then something huge happened.

My mom got a phone call from Toby Jenkins, the head of the Equality Center, and he told her that they were awarding me the Carolyn Wagner Youth Leadership Award at the

Equality Gala that year. The same award Katie had been given the first night we'd ever spent together.

"This is incredible, Arin," Mom said when she broke the news. She was starting to cry a little. "I'm so proud of you! The ceremony is on April twenty-sixth, so you have some time to prepare your speech."

April 26.

The date of my second birthday—it would be my two-year anniversary of starting testosterone. The universe was telling me that I was on the right path.

I started laughing and told her about the coincidence. "And you know what else? That's the same night as my senior prom. I guess I'm gonna miss it, and I can't say I'm too upset, after what happened at my first prom."

Spring break was coming up, and despite the disastrous trip to Colorado the year before, I really wanted to go back, but to go mountain climbing instead of skiing. Mom agreed to let me take a couple of friends. Jamie couldn't make it, so I asked Katie and my cousin Amanda to come along. Katie was understandably hesitant at first, but we'd been getting along as friends so much better since the whole Bruce Weber and Barneys campaign. We were also flown back to New York for the launch party at the beginning of February, and while it was bizarre to get thrust into the spotlight once again, there was such an outpouring of love and support from the trans community that I let myself fully enjoy it. There was a huge picture of my face in one of the windows at Barneys, and it cracked me up to wonder about what all my former child pageant judges would think of it—if they'd be proud or horrified. At any rate, maybe all of that ridiculous training had paid off after all.

I met up with Austin for dinner at a Panda Express to catch up after I got back from the New York trip, and I was riding so high on self-confidence from that and the upcoming award that before I even knew what I was doing, I blurted out that I liked him.

I watched his face for a reaction. He shifted uncomfortably in his seat and accidentally kicked the base of the table so that everything on it shook.

"Sorry. I just don't think I'm really in a place to get into anything," he said.

I felt myself crash a little inside. I couldn't help but think that it was really because I was trans—that once again I was getting rejected for not having the right thing between my legs. But I wasn't going to let it get me down. I'd come too far for that.

"I really want to stay friends, though," he said quickly.

"I do too. Hey, actually, I'm going to Colorado for spring break with a bunch of friends, to go mountain climbing. Want to come along?"

"Sure," he said. "That sounds like a lot of fun."

I felt really proud of myself for not letting the rejection affect me more. Sure, it stung, but I felt like I was growing up and getting a better handle on my emotions. I could totally be just friends with Austin. No problem.

I got a text from him the following night: *I can't really keep this back anymore. I do like you. More than just friends. I want to grab your face and kiss you.*

His initial hesitation had nothing to do with me being trans. And it had nothing to do with him not being ready to get into a relationship—it turned out that he was worried that *I* wasn't. He knew how much Katie had meant to me, and he didn't want to be a rebound fling. But I knew that what I felt for him was something that had nothing to do with my past with Katie. I couldn't wait to get to Colorado.

The trip seemed like a dream. Everyone got along with one another so well, and we climbed huge mountains, taking tons of pictures of the almost alien landscapes, full of jagged points that tried to puncture the sky. I never got any alone time with Austin, since Katie and Amanda were always with us, but that was okay. Everything felt right.

The four of us shared a hotel room, and on the last night there, *Brokeback Mountain* was on TV. I was in one bed with Katie, and Austin and Amanda were in the other bed across from us. Katie and Amanda eventually drifted off, and through the flickering light of the television screen, I saw Austin watching me from the other bed. The movie was nearing its heartbreaking end, and the beautifully sad and simple guitar music floated through the room. Austin slowly reached his arm out toward me, and we fell asleep holding hands across the open space between us.

I sat with Austin in the backseat during the second half of the nearly ten-hour drive back to Tulsa. I wanted to kiss him so bad, and I could tell he wanted to as well, but we both understood that it wasn't the right place. We wanted to be respectful of Katie. Even though she had broken up with me, it still seemed rude to flaunt our feelings in front of her. So we relied instead on dumb games like Jell-O, where we'd pretend we had no bones in our bodies and couldn't stay in place whenever we rounded a curve in the road. It's a really immature—but super convenient—way to snuggle up to someone you like while pretending you're just fooling around.

Once it grew dark, I leaned over all the way and rested my head in his lap. The outline of his face was reflected in the moonlight and he absentmindedly played with my hair. I turned forward to face the front seat, and when Katie wasn't looking, I felt him quickly but gently kiss the back of my neck.

Hours later, I woke up and stretched. The whole horizon line was pink, and the sun was just starting to rise.

"We're home," Austin whispered, and squeezed my hand.

One month later I found myself in a rented black tuxedo, walking across a massive platform toward a podium. There were huge spotlights creating white spots in my eyes, but I still managed to glimpse my mom off to the side, and I waved to her, just like I had when I'd been dressed as a baby duck as a three-year-old—my very first time on a stage. I remembered how incredibly uncomfortable I had been in that blindingly yellow leotard, feathers flying everywhere, getting in my eyes. My mom had stood and cheered for me as Emerald then, and she was still standing and cheering for me now as Arin.

Katie was standing on the stage too, along with all the other past recipients of the Youth Leadership Award, and as I passed her, we shared a small smile, silently acknowledging everything we'd been through together. As supportive as my mom had been, and as incredible as Taylor Burns was, I'm not sure that without Katie I would have come to terms with who I am as fast as I did. Despite the fact that she'd moved on to want something new, we'd still lost our virginities to each other, and there is no way that experience would have been the same if it had been with someone who didn't implicitly understand all of the tangled feelings that come with being trapped in the wrong body, but still wanting to use it to express love. She'd taught me how to not be afraid.

But our relationship was also bigger than that. It was bigger than either of us. We'd been given a chance to tell the world who we are, and it was something that neither of us ever would have accomplished just on our own. We'd been able to give hope to other trans teenagers out there. And even though, by the end, we'd been just going through the motions, it had been our union that had helped humanize us to some people who hadn't understood what it means to be trans. If nothing else, people can relate to love.

And love is messy. It can hurt so deeply that people kill over it. It can be so overpowering that you forget that everyone else in the world around you even exists. And maybe the only truth about love is that you can never, ever know where it will take you. None of those ideas are new. But nothing compares to the pain of first comprehending them.

When I reached the podium, I felt an incredible sense of

calm take over. Somewhere out there in the crowd, I knew Andi was clapping, and that Austin was watching me and sending strength. We'd been dating since the Colorado trip, and he'd been nothing but caring and sweet. My body dysphoria disappeared when I was with him. What we felt for each other transcended my physicality and made me as comfortable as I'd been in the beginning with Katie. Just the day before, he'd hugged me and said, "I like you so much, I'd climb a mountain for you. Oh, wait. I already did!"

Austin had even transferred to the same college that I'd just been accepted to, where I'd be studying psychology. I know that we're still young, that anything can happen, but everything was perfectly balanced in that one moment onstage.

Maybe I'll end up with him for good, though. Or maybe I'll end up back together with Katie one day when we're older, like she once said. Maybe I'll end up with another trans woman. Maybe I'll end up with a trans guy, or a cisgender man or woman. Maybe I'll adopt kids one day, with a husband or a wife, or even on my own.

All I do know is that I live in a fast-changing world of increasing trans acceptance, where so many options and doors that were never there before are suddenly opening. I've been blessed with a crazy amount of love in my life, and I've got so, so much to give back in return.

I looked out at the sea of people, took a deep breath, and began to speak.

ACKNOWLEDGMENTS

You know how some toys come in a box that reads SOME ASSEMBLY REQUIRED? I can relate to those toys. That phrase— "some assembly required"—really resonates with me. It captures this sense that I've had for a long time, that if I were going to be who I wanted to be, I was going to have to literally put myself together piece by piece. I had been given a physical body that didn't match my gender identity. So, I found a "manual" (thank you yet again, Internet!) and started the assembly. Most people are given a body that matches how they feel on the inside. I was not. Over the past few years I have slowly made some of the physical changes needed so that my body matches who I am on the inside.

The first and most important person who helped me do this was my mom. It is hard to articulate just how important she is to me and my journey. She gave me the support I needed and pulled me through the darkness. Without her love and understanding, this book would not be in your hands. *I* wouldn't be here today if it weren't for her.

My dad taught me how to ride everything I rode, starting with my first electric four-wheeler, with full helmet and chest protector. I thank him for being my protector and for always making things fun, no matter what.

My little brother Wesley . . . where do I even start? The

comedian and entertainer of the family. Even on the darkest days, he could always put a smile on my face. He has taught me how to laugh at myself. He's the person in my family who accepted me the fastest, and I love him infinitely.

My Gigi and Papa were part of my core foundation and gave me unconditional love through it all, constantly reiterating the values that my mom taught me, and giving me tons of encouragement to be who I am, to hold steady and always do the right thing. Always and forever, I will love them both.

Then there is Aunt Susan, my second mom and number one cheerleader. Oh, and my "agent," too—I almost forgot. I could always count on her to bring some sparkle to my day.

Of course, I need to thank Katie. She understood me when no one else could. She was there at the beginning of my transition, and we shared all of the happy and triumphant moments of watching my body change into the one I have today.

Thank you, Darian, for being there for me and making me feel human when no one else did.

I would like to also acknowledge Skylar Kergil, aka Skylarkeleven. I found him on YouTube, and he is the guy who introduced the transgender world to me. He gave me the answers and hope I was searching for. He has helped so many people with his channel and inspired me to video blog my journey as well. Many thanks to my new friend.

I don't want to leave anyone out, so I will just give thanks to the following people who taught me about how to be a friend, a survivor, a leader, and a bro: Samuel, Kennedy, Hannah

W., Butch, Kelsey, Hannah C., and my cousins Dewayne, Amanda, and Cheyenne.

I haven't mentioned my best friend yet. Andi Ullrich gave me something growing up that no one else did, and that was acceptance. She never made me feel like the weird kid, and I love her for that more than she will ever know.

My transition would not have been as smooth without the help of my therapist, Taylor Burns. Thank you for leading the way, Taylor.

A big thanks must also be given to Toby Jenkins and the Dennis R. Neill Equality Center for all that you do for the thousands who come to you yearly for support.

Christian Trimmer, my editor—without him this never would have happened. Thank you for believing my story was worth telling and for making a difference in so many lives. Thanks also to Justin Chanda, Laurent Linn, Michelle Leo, Katy Hershberger, and all of the other awesome people at Simon & Schuster.

Last but not least, my friend and cowriter, Joshua Lyon. He has given me a voice to tell my experiences with color. He has been there for an important part of my journey and has become the big brother I never had. So, Josh, thank you.

HOW TO TALK TO YOUR NEW TRANSGENDER FRIEND

(A VERY BRIEF GUIDE)

Talking with someone new is always a little tricky. But chatting with someone who is transgender can feel intimidating—we're not taught the words or "rules" to handle these conversations. I've learned that a lot of people will avoid talking to someone who is transgender because they're worried about being disrespectful. That's actually really nice. But if we're going to bridge gaps, we need to have the conversation. Hopefully, this little guide will help.

1. Don't refer to me as a "he-she" or "it." Do accept me as a full-fledged member of the gender with which I identify.
2. Don't ask me what my previous name was or say "Back when you were Fred . . ." or "When you were Linda . . ." Do use the name I go by now when speaking to me and referencing stories.
3. Don't keep using the wrong pronouns and name during someone's transition. Do try your best to remember and just correct yourself if you mess up. It happens sometimes, but as long as we know you are trying, that means everything to us.

4. Don't ask me what is in my pants, and I won't ask what is in yours. Do understand that not everyone who is a trans guy or trans girl wants sex reassignment surgery.

5. Don't talk about when I "switched" or "changed" genders. Do use "transition" to describe what I am going through or went through.

6. Don't assume I am here to shock anyone or get attention. Do believe that I just want to live a healthy, happy life and one that is true to my honest gender.

7. Don't assume that if I'm a trans guy, then I like only girls, or if I'm a trans girl, then I like only guys. Do know that gender and sexuality—which is about who you are attracted to sexually—are completely separate issues.

8. Don't be afraid to ask questions. For real, please ask questions! Do make sure the person is an openly trans person before doing so in public.

9. Don't call me every time you see that a documentary about transgender people is going to be on TV. I already know what being transgender is about! Do call me if you see a listing for something you know that I'm genuinely interested in.

10. Don't ever call a non-transsexual guy a "real guy" or "complete guy." Do know that a transgender person has done a lot of soul-searching to figure out if he or she is male or female. As such, we consider ourselves very real and totally complete.

Please use this as a general guideline; everyone experiences gender a little differently, so do your best to respect the wants and needs of the person you're hanging out with. Remember, ask questions! (See number eight above—for real!) And don't worry about messing up—everyone does at some time or another. If you can believe it, even trans people say the wrong thing to one another every now and then. Everyone's journey is different, and we all have varying degrees of openness about that journey.

RESOURCES

Books

Admittedly, I'm not a big book reader. Once I figured out I was transgender, most of the reading and research I did was online. But the following books were really useful to me.

"Welcoming Our Trans Family and Friends: A Support Guide for Parents, Families and Friends of Transgender and Gender Non-Conforming People" (Available for free download from www.pflag.org: http://community.pflag.org/Document .Doc?id=202. It's not technically a book, but it's an awesome resource. If you're transgender, this pamphlet has everything you need to help explain *you* to your loved ones.)

The Transgender Guidebook: Keys to a Successful Transition by Anne L. Boedecker, PhD, published by CreateSpace Independent Publishing Platform, 2011 (This book is just what it says it is—a guidebook, packed with a lot of information that you can pick and choose from when you are first getting started.)

The Transgender Child: A Handbook for Families and Professionals by Stephanie A. Brill and Rachel Pepper, published by Cleis

Press, Inc., 2008 (My therapist, Taylor Burns, recommends this book to all of his transgender clients and their families.)

Helping Your Transgender Teen: A Guide for Parents by Irwin Krieger, published by Genderwise Press, 2011 (Again, this one is for the moms and dads out there and comes highly recommended by Taylor.)

The Complete Guide to Transgender in the Workplace by Vanessa Sheridan, published by ABC-CLIO, LLC, 2009 (As I get older, I may have to deal with gender issues in the workplace, so I thought I would mention this one for the older teenagers and adults who might want some guidance for job-related matters.)

Be Who You Are! by Jennifer Carr, illustrated by Ben Rumback, published by AuthorHouse, 2010 (A great book for younger kids who may be trying to figure out about or cope with being a transgender person.)

Golden Boy by Abigail Tarttelin, published by Atria Books, 2013 (You should never judge a book—or person—by its cover. The novel is about a guy who is intersexual, which is something not talked about very often. I really enjoyed this book.)

Movies

Ma Vie en Rose (1997)
Taylor Burns suggested I watch the movie—and I'm

glad he did! It's in French, and it's a really great story.

Boys Don't Cry (1999)

I'm just gonna say it, this one made me cry. It was probably the first movie I watched about being transgender. It definitely makes you think about your safety.

The Laramie Project (2002)

Supersad! The movie helped me realize how far the LGBT community has come . . . and also how much further we have to go.

Prayers for Bobby (2009)

I first saw this movie when I was questioning my sexual orientation. I really wanted my mom to watch it because of the religious aspects. We were struggling with some of the same issues as the characters in the film.

Websites

YouTube: www.youtube.com

YouTube! YouTube! YouTube! I can't tell you how many hours I spent scrolling through story after story of those who had transitioned or were transitioning before me. After watching so many videos of folks who had recorded their journeys, I was inspired to do the same for those who needed to see the process and hear that they are not alone. You can find me at Rockclimber712.

Openarms Youth Project: www.openarmsproject.org

The Dennis R. Neill Equality Center/Oklahomans for Equality: www.okeq.org

National Center for Transgender Equality: www.transequality.org

Hudson's FTM Resource Guide: www.ftmguide.org

Top Surgery FTM Surgery Network: www.topsurgery.net

Glaad Transgender Resources: www.glaad.org/transgender/resources

The Trevor Project: www.thetrevorproject.org

Gay, Lesbian, Straight Education Network: www.glsen.org

TransYouth Family Allies: www.imatyfa.org

TransActive Gender Center: www.transactiveonline.org

Gender Spectrum: www.genderspectrum.org

Parents, Families and Friends of Lesbian and Gays: www.pflag.org